In Praise of Turnings

Carol Grever's Turnings is a story of high spiritual adventure. She weaves a gorgeous tapestry from the shreds of lost identity. Her emotional intelligence shines through each experience, from becoming a Buddhist to thrilling experiences in the outdoor world to finding her passion as a writer who heals. In one of the exquisite poems interwoven with the narrative, she says "... I practice my heart's name, /grounded in rock and sky." I recommend *Turnings* wholeheartedly.

  —GAIL D. STOREY, AUTHOR OF *I Promise Not to Suffer*

In *Turnings*, Carol Grever lays bare the surprises that have shaped her life—whether good, bad, or deeply painful—as a way to explore the greater meaning implicit in her own story. Written with honesty and compassion, Grever's turnings yield rich wisdom for all.

  —SUSAN J. TWEIT, AUTHOR OF *Walking Nature Home*

Carol Grever's first book addressed a specific problem—straight wives of gay men. In these essays she takes on literally everything—life, love, loss and heartache without ever resorting to cliche or sentimentality. Even better, she leaves the reader uplifted, sensing that there's always a path, always a way forward.

  —JERRIE HURD, PHOTOGRAPHER/AUTHOR OF
  THREE NOVELS, SHORT STORIES

With sometimes brutal directness, interspersed with her insightful and thoughtful poetry, Grever retraces a path from her old life to her new one, always seeking truth, deeper understanding and spiritual awareness. *Turnings* is engaging and engrossing, difficult to put down and impossible to ignore.

—DOUGLAS D. HAWK, NOVELIST

Mine is a steady diet of books. Some feed my curiosity, others taste bland. But Carol Grever's *Turnings: Reflections on a Conscious Life* nourishes my soul. More than simply an engaging read, this book is a refreshing take on transcending life's challenges and living more fully.

—MARYJO FAITH MORGAN, WRITER AND BUSINESS OWNER

Carol will become your friend as you explore with her the events that changed the course of her life. Read it all the way through, or dip into a story now and again, and ponder her poetry. As you explore Carol's life, you will be drawn to contemplate more fully the turnings that have influenced your own.

—ELEANOR A. HUBBARD, SOCIOLOGIST,
CO-EDITOR OF *Trans-Kin*

Turnings

Also by Carol Grever

Nonfiction

My Husband Is Gay
A Woman's Guide to Surviving the Crisis

When Your Spouse Comes Out
A Straight Mate's Recovery Manual

Memory Quilt
A Family Narrative

Poetry

Glimpses
A Memoir in Poetry

Sun of a New Dawn

Turnings

Reflections on a Conscious Life

Carol Grever

Dedicated to all my teachers,
who lightened and enlightened my path.

Contents

PREFACE

EAR CREEK IS A LITTLE STREAM TRICKLING ALONG THE Mesa Trail in the foothills near my Boulder home. It sings its placid song down a steep grade, then pools in a wider spot near the trail. With shade from the pine forest and smooth rocks for seats, this bend in the creek is a welcome resting place on the seven-mile hike from Chautauqua Park to Eldorado Springs. Small pebbles and smooth river rocks shine in the creek bed, clearly illumined in summer sun. Short gusts of wind ruffle the pool's surface. Wavelets pop up, then flow back, as the stream hurries on down the hill.

This creek is a metaphor for my life's episodes, times in which experiences form, emerge, crest, and dissipate, making way for the next memorable event. Like waves and currents in the stream, these experiences appear discrete, separate in themselves. But they are not. Waves come, then go, and they are always really just water. Similarly, even the most significant personal events are simply segments of the larger stream of a lifetime. The events pass, but their memories remain. Beneath the current in Bear Creek, smooth pebbles drop and linger on the bottom of the stream, just like our memories.

This book recounts my own shining pebbles, turning points that changed the direction of this life. For the past twenty years, I've been writing about straight spouse recovery. Originally, I wrote to understand and heal my own wounds by documenting the experiences of others in mixed-orientation marriages. My books and blog and documentary reveal pivotal crises and recovery stories of dozens of other people in this situation. My own history as a straight spouse mirrors theirs, though I habitually avoided disclosing much personal information.

In the early days, there were few books on this taboo topic— but not so today. People who find themselves in mixed-orientation partnerships now have many resources for help. The Internet is rich with online support groups and nonprofit organizations that serve straight spouse needs. I've done what I could in the field, and it is satisfying to know that I tried to increase understanding and bring comfort to readers. Now, that work is coming to a close. At last, it feels appropriate to explore my own turning points in greater detail, episodes previously only suggested in my poetry.

I titled this more personal book *Turnings*, because each chapter focuses on a pivotal event that turned my life in a different direction. It offers brief glimpses of experiences that replay repeatedly in my reverie. These memories are my significant pebbles, still lying on the bottom of life's stream. Finally, I can reach through time and retrieve them, wet and gleaming in the sunshine of peaceful aging. May the insights of each be useful.

— CAROL GREVER

Revelation

MELLOW LIGHT FROM THE SETTING SUN SLANTS across the budding roses. I dig at weeds in the raised bed, too nervous to do nothing. My thoughts rivet on Jim, as I replay every word of last night's argument. He's already out with a realtor, looking at rental apartments. Glancing up the hill as a car passes, I wonder if he's finally come home. The car keeps going.

I didn't mean to push it this far when I brought up a trial separation. Filled with apprehension, I stab at another dandelion. Wearily, I sit on the garden wall, my back to the waning sunset. In the lower garden, the grove of mountain ash and the cottonwoods by the creek have just leafed out. My usual anticipation of spring gardening is dim this year. I'm too worried.

Jim has been gone for hours. I wonder if he's found his "bachelor pad." I wonder if he's found another woman! In the fading light, I hear his car door slam. Jim comes through the gate, looking drawn and tense. In silence, he slumps down beside me. For a long time, neither of us speaks. Finally, he faces me squarely, nervous and shaken.

"I don't want to leave." His voice lowers to a whisper, "But I have to."

Jim's earlier enthusiasm has drained away. The excitement he showed last night is gone. Instead, he looks scared and beaten. Seeing his torment, I feel a familiar rush of tenderness.

"I don't understand. I thought you *wanted* to leave me. You seemed anxious to move." Jim seems to shrink into the growing darkness. He slowly shakes his head, eyes closed.

"I found an apartment today, but when it was time to sign the lease, I just couldn't do it." I wait. At last, Jim finally tells me the tip of his truth, the shadowy secret he's hidden through our thirty years of marriage. His words are constricted, his voice strained and unfamiliar.

"I have homosexual tendencies."

Boom! "Homosexual." After a searing moment of shock, my mind spins around this startling confession. With that one vast understatement, everything in my life shifts. I can't fully comprehend it. I can only glimpse the terrible cost of his secret in his anguished face. His identity hidden in lies and half-truths, he has been as isolated as I. This is the husband I never really knew.

For the first time in all our years together, Jim cries piteous, pent-up tears. Watching him convulse with sobs, I open my arms in shared sorrow, holding him close. I'm thoroughly confused, but somehow I feel strangely relieved. There isn't another woman. It isn't about me!

Hanging Together

Weeks passed after that astonishing revelation in the spring of 1991. Jim and I processed mountains of information and emotions, vacillating between despair and hope. We had so much to lose, I thought somehow we might accommodate our differences—as long as he promised to stop lying to me. I demanded total honesty. We talked and talked. But as the naked truth about his past and present gradually unfolded, it became clear that he not only had "homosexual tendencies." He was actively engaged in secret same-sex encounters – and had been during most of our married life.

It honestly had never, ever occurred to me that Jim hid *any* secrets, much less that he lived this lie each day of his adult life. How could I have missed such a fundamental fact? Surely he left clues. I must have been blind and stupid to live in the dark all those years! If I had been on an emotional roller coaster before, now I was in for the ride of my life.

As days went by, my stress became unbearable. My dad's losing battle with leukemia added layers of tension. Still holding Jim's secret, I frequently flew to Tulsa to help my parents during their overwhelming burden. Home alone, Jim's changes and sexual activity accelerated. His physical transformation was obvious—a jazzed-up appearance, dyed hair and beard, flashy clothes and an expensive new convertible. He joined a men's group with younger friends whom I didn't know.

My tipping point came when Jim decided to go alone on a trip we'd planned together. I sat in Tulsa, grieving in my father's hospital room, while Jim flew alone to Hawaii for a corporate convention and vacation. It was infuriating to picture him sunning on a beach, half a world away, especially when I desperately needed his emotional support. There had been a lot of loneliness in our married life, but that set a new record. I was wounded to the core.

It only got worse at home after that. Hardest of all, I had to keep *everything* secret from *everyone*. Jim and I went to work and social events as usual, and I lied with every breath. Every family conversation was cloaked in untruth. To the outer world, nothing had changed, but I was smothering in the closet with Jim, confined and alone.

My Dad died on July 8, just five weeks after Jim's disclosure. I flew back to Tulsa just in time. My mother and I held each of Daddy's hands, giving him gentle permission to let go of his valiant struggle. He died peacefully, with the same dignity he'd carried through life and through his final, awful illness. He had always been my role model and my greatest ally—my hero. I was devastated. My grief was a black, bottomless hole. Within one year, I had lost the three men I'd loved most in my life—my father, Jim's father, and Jim himself. All the tears I'd dammed behind a strong will and foolish optimism gushed through this valley of loss. When Daddy died, I cried and cried, thinking I'd never stop.

Back in Boulder, Jim and I struggled to stay together. Jim wanted an open marriage. Our arrangement was that either of us could go out with other men, provided we kept no secrets from each other. It worked for him. Jim simply continued as before, widening his circle of gay friends. After an evening out, he'd come back flushed with excitement, keen to talk about his experiences. Increasingly isolated, I stayed at home. Though I had "permission" to pursue pleasure with others, I lacked the energy and nerve. Actually, I was terrified by the prospect. So I worked days and stayed home alone at night.

As autumn turned to winter, I grew resentful that Jim had everything he wanted—and I did not. I languished while he relished his double life ever more actively, his secret sexual exploits cloaked by our long-term marriage. Lies and half-truths were a daily necessity, as we continued to work together in our business, pretending to have an ideal marriage. I still couldn't speak honestly with anyone, not even my own mother. There was no security anywhere, and the inequity of the situation finally became intolerable. My greatest fear had always been to be absolutely alone, and now that seemed inevitable.

While I imagined that Jim was having a gay old time, he was also suffering. Our marriage did shield him from society's judgment, but he was not free to express himself fully as a gay man. Like me, he was hiding behind lies, fearful of a lonely future. Our decades together had made us codependent. His ambivalence grew as his gay support groups urged him to make the break.

We were both in therapy, and I felt absolutely crazy. I was frightened by my wild mood swings. I had to find a way to heal myself, and I desperately needed spiritual support. Searching for relief, I tried sitting meditation. My position as a trustee of Naropa University had awakened an interest in Tibetan Buddhist teachings. I enrolled in thirteen Shambhala Training meditation weekends over the next months and set out on a fresh spiritual path.

We had really tried to make our open arrangement work, but I finally looked in the mirror and said, "What about me? What's my future in this?" Ultimately, I understood that I couldn't spend the rest of my days accommodating someone else's needs at the expense of my own. I had to create a new life for myself. I had to face my fear of loneliness and end this unequal marriage. That insight set me on a path to precarious freedom.

Slow-Motion Separation

Dismantling a life takes time! Our complex business, investments, home, office building, and all our possessions had been jointly earned and were jointly held. We had spent more than thirty years creating this shared life. I grieved its termination like a death. Our slow, complicated separation did have one unexpected advantage. It gave us time to process overwhelming change in a subtler way. Immense patience was required to extricate ourselves, especially since we were determined not to harm each other further. Still, the stress of uprooting everything familiar was wrenching. With some wrong turns, one mediated confrontation about fair shares, and a stroke of luck, we found a buyer, closed the sale of our business, and divided our assets and property.

Over those two final years we spent in the same house, secretly preparing to separate, divesting ourselves of our property and business interests, I continued my spiritual quest. I participated in the whole series of weekend meditation programs at the Shambhala Center. Sitting still in deep meditation, I felt my bruised, vulnerable heart in a new way. The psychic underpinnings of the practice allowed me to work with my personal situation as it unfolded, meeting it with growing courage. Buddhist teachings emphasized calm abiding, recognizing the interconnectedness of all sentient beings, while striving to do no harm.

On July 2, 1994, I took action on what I'd known in my heart for many months. I took refuge in the Buddha, the Dharma, and the Sangha—the teacher, the teachings, and the spiritual community. I became a Buddhist. By then, I recognized that Jim and I were not so different in our pain. Just like me, he needed an authentic life. It was an act of love to let him go. Our protracted process actually offered an advantage: spiritually, I became prepared for our separation.

Before he moved from our home, Jim determined to come out to all our family. I had suffocated in the closet of secrecy, so I was relieved that I could at last speak honestly. I encouraged Jim to be completely open. Besides, without knowing the whole truth, how could any of them ever understand our "sudden" separation? We traveled together to visit each relative in person. We told Jim's mother first, then flew to Oklahoma and California to see my mother and our two sons. Jim was panic-stricken, but I stood behind him through each frightful conversation. My overriding emotion was deep grief.

Telling Jim's mother was hardest, especially when her response was, "I'd rather have heard that you were dying." But after her shock subsided, over time, she accepted and even embraced the facts. Others in the family seemed less harsh. Our younger son commented that he had lots of gay friends and that this disclosure was not a problem for him. I was pleased and surprised by his brother's response: "Dad, there's nothing you could ever do that would make me stop loving you." After delivering each revelation, Jim felt released, and I felt free!

Soon after telling the family, Jim bought a condominium in another part of town and moved there the spring before our business sale was finalized. I remained at "Treehouse," comforted by our home's warm familiarity, my healing garden, and my beloved cat, Sundance. A few months later, I filed for divorce. It was helpful that we had already settled our financial shares during the business sale. That settlement enabled us to use the same divorce attorney and to maintain civility throughout the procedure. We were determined to salvage as much friendship as we could, honoring our long history together and the preciousness of our remaining family ties. Our attorney said that ours was the most amicable case he'd ever handled. Our divorce was final in April 1996, five years after Jim's initial disclosure to me of his homosexual orientation. Our marriage lasted thirty-five years.

Stones

In darkness
he'd held them always.
Hiding in his closet
he filled his secret sack,
bravado wrapping reality.
I stood outside,
shielded by ignorance
while he added
stone after stone
to that bag.
Each one a lie,
told and retold
till he believed himself.

Intimations of truth
pulled me in
to share his shadow.
Night and day melded
as we huddled there
a long, long time.

Slowly, he emptied his sack
now too heavy to bear.
One by one,
he gave stones to me.
Stone after stone shifted
from his bag to mine.

I could barely lift the load
when at last
he cracked the closet door.
Sudden sunshine flooded
light on his empty sack,
mine, full of stones.

It took years to dole them out,
one for each friend,
each loved one, betrayed.
No life escapes pain.
I still carry
a pocketful of pebbles.
Memories don't die
but my bag for secrets
is folded and flat,
finally empty.

Cradle of Wisdom

"THIS IS A FOREIGN COUNTRY!"

That was my first thought upon entering the Lincoln Building, a converted elementary school that housed Boulder's Naropa Institute. No students were in sight, that late Monday afternoon in 1990. I had come to meet Dale Asrael, a professor of religious studies, recommended to me as an outstanding teacher. I hoped that she would agree to guide my independent study in Buddhist meditation practices.

Before, I had merely driven past this unusual campus. Walking into the main building took me out of Boulder and into Tibet. The reception area was deserted, dominated by a giant painting of the Wheel of Dharma on the wall. A subtle scent of incense filled the air. In a classroom on my right, instead of student desks, dark blue meditation cushions lined the floor in neat rows. Passing through a quiet hall to my appointment, I paused to study an intricate Thangka painting, a depiction of what appeared to be a goddess. I later learned that it was an image of Tara, the Tibetan ideal of compassion. Everything in this strange school offered a taste of Tibet, thriving incongruously in the middle of a trendy Colorado city.

The smells, the colors, the foreign atmosphere were exotic and intriguing. I had no idea on that day that Naropa would change my future life.

My former ties to the Christian church and to Unity had frayed, and my childhood religion no longer seemed relevant. Feeling restless and dissatisfied, I needed a fresh start and came to Naropa to experiment with a different spiritual practice. I was curious about this Buddhist-inspired college that combined contemplative studies with traditional Western scholastic and artistic disciplines. I knew little of Buddhism at the time, but Naropa was the obvious place to learn more.

Aside from an opportunity to pursue philosophy, it was exciting to return to a small, liberal arts campus, recalling my faculty years at Phillips University in Enid. It evoked my academic roots, though in a totally dissimilar environment. The contrast between the two institutions was striking. Phillips was a seventy-five-year-old conventional Christian Church-affiliated university that embodied conservative American religious values. Naropa was a wildly edgy, avant-garde institute, Buddhist based, still not officially accredited as a university.

The college began as a simple summer institute in 1974, founded by Chögyam Trungpa Rinpoche, a maverick monk who escaped to India after the Chinese invasion of Tibet, then studied at Oxford in England. Charismatic teachers, led by Trungpa and Ram Dass, set out to introduce Eastern religious concepts in the Rocky Mountain West. They expected perhaps two hundred students that first summer in Boulder, but they were stunned by an enrollment of two thousand. It was a motley young crowd, disenchanted with the Vietnam war and crass materialism, and disengaged from mainline society.

Many found inspiration that summer in Trungpa's eccentric and controversial presentation of the dharma. This teacher was their kindred spirit: a brilliant nonconformist, rebelling against convention, bringing an entirely new approach to ancient Tantric wisdom.

From this unlikely beginning, an alternative college emerged, named for Naropa (1016-1100), one of the best-known Indian master teachers at the Buddhist monastic university, Nalanda. Boulder's Naropa Institute, later accredited as Naropa University, attracted bright, committed, exceptional students, imbued with Buddhist idealism and a desire to serve mankind. Naropa's history and environment intrigued me because I was already questioning my conventional middle-class attitudes and religion. In the midst of existential angst, I needed a fresh identity. This alien establishment offered a new approach to spiritual practice based on a different world-view. In short order, I gratefully slipped into Naropa's engaging culture.

The timing of my introduction to Buddhism and Naropa was fortuitous. One encounter on the campus illustrates the auspicious nature of that engagement. A few weeks after Jim came out, I sat on a bench outside the Lincoln Building, feeling deep sadness over the upending of my formerly carefree life. Wiping tears, I looked up into the calm, clear face of one of Trungpa's original students who had remained at the school as a teacher of improvisational dance.

"I'm falling apart," I sighed.

Gently taking my hand, she encouraged me in just the way I needed at that moment.

"I think, if you have to fall apart, Naropa is the best place to be." With encouraging words and a sympathetic smile, she continued on to her waiting class. It was a reminder that this was a place to explore one's true nature. It was acceptable to feel lost here, knowing that others would understand and support growth.

Inspired by Buddhist principles of nonviolence, compassion, wisdom, and service, I continued to read and practice at Naropa, guided by my meditation instructor, Dale Asrael. Tibetan sitting meditation became part of my routine, along with weekend meditation retreats to study the Shambhala curriculum.

Right away, I discovered that these studies required familiarity with many Sanskrit, Pali, and Tibetan words. In my early days there, I was exposed to dozens of foreign expressions, freely tossed about in any campus conversation. At first, I felt slightly offended by these unfamiliar words that seemed to be shibboleths to exclude outsiders. As a newcomer, I wanted to fit in. I determined to learn more of this new vocabulary. My tattered copy of *The Shambhala Dictionary of Buddhism and Zen* attests to that focused study.

Though frustrated in the beginning, I slowly understood that these words are useful and precise. They became an essential part of my own vocabulary, and now seem like old friends. One example is the Tibetan name of my favorite teacher, Pema Chödrön. *Pema* means *Lotus*, symbol of awakened mind or enlightenment; *Chodron* means *Dharma Torch*, a fiery light illuminating the teachings of the Buddha. Her name is a perfect description of her lifelong work as a Buddhist nun and dharma teacher. Like any terminology of specialized fields, such words serve as shorthand to encompass complex concepts.

By 1992, I was invited to join the Naropa Board of Trustees and was received with enthusiasm. With my business career winding down, I welcomed this fresh challenge. The highly engaged board was seriously demanding, particularly in the area of financial development. I was ready for the task and chaired the fundraising committee. After our staffing company sold, I became even more deeply involved at Naropa and served a three-year term as Chairman of the Board. It was worthy work over a total of eleven years, an arduous, absorbing commitment with life-altering effects. The principled Buddhist philosophy became my passion, and I studied diligently before taking the Refuge Vow to "do no harm."

Naropa offered grounding and acceptance and meaning when I felt lost. It became my spiritual community. For that, I remain deeply indebted and connected. Though remaining an ally of the university, I gradually gravitated away from the guru-centric Tibetan Shambhala teachings to the Middle Way of the Mahayana. Inspired by Pema Chödrön and studies of eighth-century root texts by Shantideva, I deepened that Mahayana connection in 2008 by taking the *Bodhisattva* (Enlightenment Being) Vow. Acharya Dale Asrael presided over the ceremony held at Karma Dzong, Boulder's Buddhist temple. I vowed to "exchange self for other" and to devote my life to service.

Making conscious choices involving human service, I resonate with the Dalai Lama's assertion that "My religion is kindness." I have become an avid volunteer, teaching fitness to seniors at the YMCA, leading dharma book studies, taking leadership roles in my Rotary club, and funding non-profit service initiatives and organizations. For me, this answers the question posed by poet Mary Oliver: *Tell me, what is it you plan to do with your one wild and precious life?*

My engagement with Naropa University opened my heart and mind to the teachings of the Buddha. In its cradle of wisdom, I discovered a remedy for my deepest emotional wound and undertook a crash course in basic philosophic expression. Sitting meditation remains my central practice, a quest for wisdom and compassion its foundation. The day I first walked onto the Naropa campus, I was a blank tablet, a curious newcomer, utterly unfamiliar with Tibetan or Buddhist traditions. I had no idea that Naropa would provide a fundamental turning point that would redirect all my remaining years.

Conversion

Rocky Mountain Dharma Center, 1994

Alone in my tent, huddled in my summer sleeping bag, I wait through a long night. Over and over, I lift the window flap to peer at the ominous orange glow behind the next mountain ridge. Wildfires still reflect on layers of smoke in pre-dawn darkness, the acrid smell drifting into the tent. Everyone here at Rocky Mountain Dharma Center is on edge, alert, ready to evacuate should the winds carry the fire over that nearby ridge. I lie back down on the cot, cover my nose with the blanket, and stare into the dark.

I've come to this camp, along with a dozen others, to take Refuge Vows with Sakyong Mipham Rinpoche, assisted by the Buddhist nun I've come to love as my teacher, Ani Pema Chödrön. This is a momentous step for me, a lifelong Christian, brought up in a conservative Oklahoma church. It is a significant marker, the aftermath of the biggest turning point in my life.

When Jim laid bare his "homosexual tendencies" after our thirty years of marriage, his understated revelation was a shock.

I already knew that he was pulling away from me, but I didn't know why until that Memorial Day in 1991. I had already left the church of my childhood, losing that spiritual guide. My life was in chaos; I stood alone and scared.

That is how I was thrust firmly onto this new Buddhist path. When Jim came out, I had already read several introductory books on Buddhist teachings and had begun to practice sitting meditation. Pema's first book, *The Wisdom of No Escape,* inspired me to enroll in a week-long retreat at Rocky Mountain Dharma Center. There, I could learn directly from her. Receiving her teachings in the shrine tent, I hung on every word and felt strong connection, though we hadn't met personally. On the third day of the retreat, I timidly wrote a request for a private meeting. I was thrilled when her reply soon appeared on the camp message board, inviting me to her cabin to talk. Now in 1994, three years have passed since that memorable meeting. In the smoky solitude of my tent, I vividly recall every detail.

Walking up the dusty, winding mountain road from "downtown" at the center of the camp, I tremble with nervousness and anticipation. Surely this wise woman can offer succor and guidance during my crisis. Like most straight spouses whose mates have come out, I'm bombarded by a barrage of confusing emotions—from shock and rage to sympathy for my husband's necessity to deceive. At first I denied the reality of our situation, hoping he could change. More often, I've fallen into the dark hole of grief and loss, alternately blaming him and myself. My confidence and identity are lost.

Amid a dissonance of conflicting thoughts, I arrive at Pema's cabin and knock. A household helper ushers me into the sitting room where I bow and take my seat in a chair facing Pema. At last we meet in person. Her presence is magnetic, her kind face wreathed in that famous warm smile. My tension eases as she draws out my story with gentle encouragement. She assures me that sometimes "having the rug pulled out" can be "good news." The ensuing chaos can be a gateway to something better. Her calming words offer hope.

That initial conversation with Pema confirmed my new direction. After our meeting, I pursued the dharma with beginner's mind and fresh enthusiasm. Now, after three years of regular practice and study, I'm finally ready to embrace Buddhism officially.

Daylight comes at last. The camp has made it through the fire danger without need to evacuate. I roll up my sleeping bag in cold morning light and prepare for the Refuge Ceremony. I'm excited, but nervous. In the Tibetan tradition, I'll receive a dharma name from the Sakyong, the presiding monk. What symbolic name will he give me? I've heard that whatever name he chooses may seem confusing at first, but its deeper significance will become clearer through dedicated study and meditation.

The sun is brilliant now, smoky haze lifting, last night's wildfire apparently contained. Our dignified ceremony will proceed in the shrine tent at the center of camp. The ritual has three stages: a teaching on the meaning of refuge, the recitation of refuge vows, and the giving of a new name to each "refugee." After sitting meditation and inspiring words from the Sakyong, the group collectively vows to do no harm, sealed with traditional bows. We formally take refuge in the Buddha, the dharma, and the sangha. We become Buddhists.

After our formal vows, the new refugees walk solemnly to the front to receive our assigned dharma names. I bow to accept my certificate, then gaze with delight at the hand-painted calligraphy: *Pema Yudron*, Tibetan for "Lotus Turquoise Torch." I have received my teacher's name, *Pema*! It's an unspeakable honor—and lifelong responsibility. I promise myself that I will strive to be worthy of my dharma name, to be "Pema2." Our formal ceremony ends with Ani Pema throwing rice into the crowd, as at a wedding, joyously joining the celebration of our new identity.

Shambhala Mountain Center, 2015

I've come back here once again. Though the name of this remote camp has changed during the past twenty years, its original purpose has remained. I still feel at home here. These steep trails are familiar in the early morning light. How many meditative steps have stirred these rocks, imprinted this sand since that long-ago day I took refuge? I have made many of those footprints myself, returning a dozen times over the years for meditation retreats, receiving ancient wisdom from Pema Chödrön and other enlightened teachers. Today, I retrace a path I've hiked in times of grief, hope, confusion, and celebration. This time, I'm on a different quest for wisdom to guide my final years of this precious human life.

My boots crunch the gravel in the meditative rhythm of my breath. Hands folded, I wind through brilliant October aspen and towering pine. I wrap my jacket tighter. Fog hangs on granite cliffs above, sending chilly fingers into the valley. The brisk morning breeze dances through tall grass by the trail.

Abundant life is all around. Unafraid, a cottontail rabbit crosses my path, as a black-striped ground squirrel skitters into the brush. Halfway up the hill, the trail takes a sharp left turn leading to a curved wooden bridge. Spanning a whispering creek below, the bridge is shaded by golden quaking aspens, their white bark shining in the breaking sun. Fluttering Tibetan prayer flags light up the thin air.

Another bend in the trail opens a clear view of an architectural wonder. Glowing white, with a high golden dome that commands the hillside, the Great Stupa of Dharmakaya is a monument to compassion and basic goodness. Its stunning beauty is said to bring enlightenment upon a single view. In Tibetan tradition, stupas are meant to promote harmony, prosperity, longevity, good health, and peace. Sitting in the heart of Colorado's Rocky Mountains, the Great Stupa is a unique work of art with meticulous architectural detail, precisely dictated by Tibetan tradition. Inside, the massive structure is adorned with precious original statues, relics and paintings. A huge golden Buddha overlooks a circle of meditation cushions on the marble floor of the main hall. To sit here in silent contemplation is inspiring. No matter how many times I return, the Great Stupa of Dharmakaya still takes my breath.

Once again, I mindfully climb the steps approaching the imposing monument. Slowly, I circumambulate the building three times, clockwise, then remove my shoes to enter the shrine room. I sit cross-legged under the towering Buddha's realistic, open eyes. Wrapped in silence, all mundane concerns fall away.

Breathe in, breathe out. Let go of strife and care. Relax as it is, with gratitude.

I have practiced similarly for more than twenty years. Internalizing the teachings of the Buddha is my chosen path, ignited by my first encounter with Ani Pema. "Chaos can be a very good thing," Pema said. Every experience, pleasant or horrible, can be "fuel for waking up." My habitual apathy and delusion were once shattered, but core Buddhist truths were my guide to renewal. Every life event can be a step toward enlightenment.

Conversion

Wildfires spread just over the ridge.
Eerie glow flashes on black
between mountain and sky.
Can we stay through this night?
Watch the flickering skyline and wait.
Evacuation looms till winds shift
and daylight seeps through haze.

I too came through fire
burning illusion to ash.
Now the wind has changed.
Today I commit to wake up, grow up
to take a right turn, a new name.
Buddhist. Pema. Lotus.
Ambiguity wilts in hope's heat.
Merging with reality
a solitary path opens.

Wildfires subside,
but this spark glows
vivid in my open heart.

Goodbye to Temptation

I COULD DRIVE THESE ROADS IN MY SLEEP. BOULDER, TO Golden, to I-70, to Silverthorne. Cross Vail Pass, speed on to GlenwoodSprings, Palisade, then Grand Junction. Take a hard left off the interstate into the Utah desert. Pass through Moab, and wind across red hills and sandstone to Lake Powell and our boat slip at hall's crossing. I've traveled this nine-hour route many times, but this trip is unique. Instead of riding beside Jim, meeting boating friends to party away carefree days at the lake, I'm driving my mother and aunt through this spectacular beauty for their first and last time.

As the striking panorama unfolds, my passengers thrill with each change in the Rocky Mountain scenery. Their congenial chatter is soothing, and I can allow myself to look straight ahead at the road and lose myself in thought. Bittersweet memories of Lake Powell wash over me as we pass each landmark town along the way. This trip will be my farewell to the *Temptation*, our thirty-two-foot houseboat, before it is sold. Sharing it with my two eldest relatives is a high priority now, before it's too late.

This lake represents a whole segment of my life, a reward for twenty-three arduous years building our staffing business. For the past twelve of those years, it offered respite from demanding routine. A day at Powell often began with early morning skiing on glassy, undisturbed waters. We explored ancient peoples' cliff dwellings and relaxed in remote canyons. Simply floating in the sun-warmed water was heavenly pleasure. To me, Powell was more than a lake; it was the embodiment of freedom, a temporary release from ordinary care and responsibility. I used to relax with a drink on the top deck and fantasize about living full-time on the *Temptation*. This compact home on the water was a treasured retreat. Today's trip will be different. I'll say goodbye to the *Temptation* and the tranquil past that Lake Powell symbolized. It is only one loss among many, as Jim and I prepare to divorce.

Through this day of travel to the lake, Aunt Toady is enthralled by the Rockies. She catches her breath at every turn and is as excited as a child. "Oh!" she exclaims, her arm sweeping the purple-shaded horizon. "It looks like a painting!" As usual, Mama is more subdued, quieter, probably reminiscing about her relaxed road trips to Colorado with my Dad. Widowed now for a decade, her pleasure in the scenery is tinged with her own loss. Alternating anticipation and grief, I can identify with that! Still, she is also eager to see for the first time my storied Lake Powell.

By late afternoon, crossing the Utah border, we escape congested I-70 and turn onto the old State Road 128. Forested rocky peaks are far behind us now, those views replaced by hot sandstone walls, towering above sage and sand. This less-traveled route passes the ghost town of Cisco and winds alongside the Colorado River. Ours is the only car in sight. I point out distinctive formations of Arches National Park, outlined on the horizon. Today's contrast in scenery is remarkable, from deep green pines and grey granite cliffs of the mountains, to a dozen shades of red over desert flats. Soon, we'll refuel and stretch in Moab before the final leg of our journey to Hall's Crossing Marina at Lake Powell.

By sunset, we reach Hall's and pull into the marina parking area. Stiff and weary, we're excited to be here at last. First, we must carry our food and other essentials onto the dock. For the first time, I realize just how frail my mother and aunt have become. Toady is permanently bent after back surgeries, her heavy legs weakened by inactivity. Though older by eight years, Mama is tiny, more lithe, but still unsteady after the long drive. I feel a withering wave of responsibility for them here. In this remote place, we're far from help for any emergency, and I wonder if I've made a mistake in bringing them to the Utah desert. I swallow hard. Always before, I was one of several strong people on these trips. Now, I'm fully in charge.

I lead my guests to the last slip on the dock, chosen for its unobstructed views across the lake. It's a relief to see that the *Temptation* and ski boat are sound and securely moored, clean and inviting as ever. With no one to help, my challenge is lifting the heavy ice chests and bags from the walkway onto the houseboat. My ladies' big task is simply climbing the ladder, struggling just to get aboard. With encouragement and my steady arm of support, they land safely on deck. After another hour, I have our food and gear stowed.

Settling my dear tired ones in comfortable lounge chairs on the upper deck, I try to gather my courage as I organize a quick meal in the galley below. They are grateful for quiet rest, enjoying the sound of small waves lapping the dock and watching the sun drop behind dark distant cliffs across the lake.

I move pensively through the silent cabin to the cozy quarters where Jim and I slept. Our patchwork quilt on the bed, the desert painting on the wall, our swim suits in the drawer—every object holds a memory. I've clearly set myself up for melancholy this weekend, bringing along a box of family photos to sort. I'll keep some, and send others to Jim and our two sons. I shove the box under the bed to face later. Maybe when I'm not so tired. During this short two-day stay, Mama and Toady can sample brief glimpses of life on the lake, but this first night, we crave only sleep.

Morning comes too soon. I manage a cheerful, carefree front through breakfast, hiding any uncertainty. But clearly, this adventure will be challenging for my elders. Every movement is hard for them—climbing to the upper deck, getting into and out of the ski boat, simply walking on the narrow dock and crossing the gangway up to the marina. Their fear of falling is legitimate. I pray that nothing goes wrong.

I don't have the confidence to take the houseboat out of the marina, but I can manage the ski boat alone. Slow, scenic rides through lofty, red canyon walls are familiar and welcoming for me, foreign and exciting for my ladies. Still, despite years of boating experience, it's a stretch to look after two frail women engaged in such alien activities. Constantly alert, I understand why we always brought lots of friends on earlier outings at Powell.

After a hot afternoon of shopping at the marina and boating through nearby canyons, we settle back into the homey *Temptation*. The three of us crowd into the tiny galley, making much ado of cooking our simple potato soup. During the day's sightseeing, our conversation mostly centered on the boats, the lake, and the stark grandeur of the canyons. Now, the subject is about to change. As we finish washing the dishes, my aunt finally asks the question that has hung in the air through the whole trip.

"Why do you have to leave Jim? You've been together practically all your lives!" She opens her arms wide, embracing this lake and my whole history.

"Look at this beautiful boat. You're giving up a life anyone would envy." Toady's confusion is understandable. Her religious and generational rejection of divorce overshadows the fact that Jim has come out as gay. How can I help her understand? Climbing the three steps up to the living area, we settle stiffly on the sofa. This will be painful.

"Don't you see? I can't deny his deepest truth, and I can't live with endless lies and secrecy either." I'm close to tears, frustration growing. My aunt's disapproval is clear, my mother's quiet grief even more wrenching.

Mama presses the question. "Why can't you just keep this a secret—not tell anybody?"

Taking a deep breath, I try again. "Trust is broken, Mama. My risk is too great. Even though we still love each other as best we can, I won't settle for a sham marriage sheltered by lies!"

Even as I protest, I recognize that much of their confusion comes from knowing only an outline of the whole story. I won't detail Jim's decades of risky infidelity and deception or reveal my pervasive loneliness within our marriage. While their protective fear is touching, they are simply unable to comprehend how I can abandon a thirty-year marriage and start over.

One difficult conversation won't change their minds or hearts. Women in their generation with a gay spouse probably would have kept it all a dark secret, as Mama suggested, living the lie until they died. My decision to open wide this closet of secrets is a complete mystery to them. We talk a little more, but my explanations are like speaking in a foreign tongue.

At last, they give in to fatigue and settle into their beds, Toady on the sofa and Mama tucked into the cuddy below the main deck. When I'm sure that my well-meaning loved ones are asleep, I sort through those bittersweet family pictures, pausing on each one to remember a time of innocence and trust. It's heartbreaking. The center didn't hold. What I thought was real wasn't. I once believed that marriage was forever; now I cry silent tears of grief over its loss. Feeling very sorry for myself, I suddenly see clearly that I am just as frail and fragile as my mother and aunt. Like them, I am terribly afraid of falling and failing. We share the peril of passing time.

Tomorrow, we'll drive those familiar roads back to Boulder. Letting go of lovely Lake Powell and the *Temptation* is symbolic of the end of my life as I knew it. I'll miss this boat, our placid view across the lake, skiing for miles on still morning waters in canyons I know so well. I'll miss feeling secure and settled and loved. I'll miss trusting in my mate. I'll miss being a wife.

Dolphin Magic: Hunting the Dream

I WAS LOOKING FOR MAGIC. DOLPHINS HAVE DRAWN SPIRI-
tual idealists and those who love the sea since ancient
times. When an opportunity came to travel to the sheer aqua
waters of the Bahamas to swim with these graceful creatures, I
didn't hesitate. Maybe the legends are true that dolphins communicate with people to help them heal their hurts. In the
midst of my raw personal and career transition, I was open to
any possibility. Packing my snorkel gear, I had no inkling how
much this journey would teach me.

Arriving in Freeport the first week in June, I was pleased that
Grand Bahama Island is less frantic than neighboring Nassau,
the energy somehow cleaner. Though this was my first major
trip as a single woman, I tried to accept loneliness and view this
leisurely day in Lucaya as a meditative opportunity. The following day a group of strangers would board the chartered ninety-
foot dive boat for our dolphin adventure. The sea temperature

was eighty-three degrees, a smart breeze cooling the heat of dazzling sun. The hotel beach was delightfully uncrowded early in the season, though it shone like pure sugar. I savored the soothing sun. The surf seemed to breathe, the incoming tide lapping its margin, like wine filling a cup. Bodysurfing and floating alone on sparkling turquoise waves, I relaxed completely.

Spiritual Smorgasbord

This first summer after my separation, traveling alone was a challenge. I noted that the passenger list from the tour company included only one couple; the rest, like me, were apparently single women. Their addresses intrigued me: one each from Japan, Holland, England, and Switzerland, the rest scattered from New York to Florida to California. Only one other woman came from Colorado. Our diversity promised interesting conversation.

But "diversity" hardly describes it. We represented a virtual spiritual smorgasbord. This group of mostly mature women embodied a whole catalogue of New Age practices. Nodding tolerantly, we listened politely to an astonishing array of doctrines, calmly accepting each other's outrageousness as if we all made perfect sense.

One woman was solidly fixed on extraterrestrials and astrology, convinced that she came from another planet. Another claimed to channel wisdom from some ancient being. There was a tarot reader and a hairdresser who believed she had been a dolphin in a former life. Though skeptical of their uncommon worldviews, I had to admit to myself that I was also on a mystical journey with my newfound Buddhism. Despite our obvious dissimilarities, we shared two common threads: we were all walking wounded, and we all revealed a peculiar kind of expectant naïveté. Through this dolphin encounter, each of us hoped to bring light into our private pockets of darkness.

I was immediately drawn to Amaya, the shy Japanese lady. The two of us, with Jackie, a young mother, were assigned to the same sleeping quarters below deck. Dive boats are not known for creature comforts, but we were taken aback by our cramped cabin on the *Sea Fever*. Three bunks, one above the other, hung from the wall at the end. The floor space was so limited we had to take turns getting dressed. Belongings had to be stowed at the foot of each bed. I chose the top bunk, hoping to feel less confined, but my face was less than two feet from the ceiling. My claustrophobia raged. With any luck, we would spend most of our time on deck or in the water during this trip.

First Test

Our itinerary was to sail from Lucaya to West End Island, where we would spend Saturday afternoon snorkeling the reef there. The following day we would move into the open sea and spend the next four days in a shallow area a few hours out, where a large pod of dolphins could usually be found. Though our two-hour passage to West End was very rough, passengers of the *Sea Fever* were blissfully unaware of a major storm brewing to the West.

The next morning, we were told to expect heavy seas when we sailed to the dolphin grounds. Tom, the captain, strongly urged everyone on board to take medication to prevent seasickness—even if we had never experienced it before. A tropical storm had swept across Cuba during the night; the squalls we experienced earlier were just its outer fringe. Depending on the course of the storm, Tom warned that we could hit a real roller coaster in the dolphin grounds.

Hitting our first eight-foot swells, I had a nag of fear but found some comfort in the thought that this old tub had seen lots of high waves in its twenty-year history. The sea indeed looked different in the clouded morning light. Deep indigo to black, the surface appeared oily, like a viscous skin grown overnight.

As the sea grew rougher, the boat pitched wildly. The crew insisted that we all stay together *outside*. Going below would guarantee severe seasickness. We sat on the floor of the main deck, legs outstretched, huddled against the back wall and staring across the stern into curtains of rain. Conversation was impossible in the driving wind and roar of diesel engines. We were isolated, despite being packed together. My loneliness was familiar, but I yearned for peaceful waters filled with friendly dolphins.

Instead, the further we traveled, the rougher the sea became. By noon, eleven extremely seasick landlubbers littered the bare deck. Faces turned an unearthly color, something between grey and olive green. Surrounded by heaving bodies, I felt exceedingly fortunate not to be susceptible to this curse! Probably, I also escaped by meditating through most of that fateful day. I simply sat, my gaze firmly fixed on the still horizon, just as if I were on my cushion in a quiet meditation hall. Following my breath, I felt oddly peaceful, despite experiencing the worst outer tempest imaginable.

Allison Strikes

As the day dragged by, intermittent gales erased the horizon with swags of rain. I began to doubt that the crew heeded radioed weather warnings in this infamous Bermuda Triangle. Finally, in mid-afternoon, Captain Tom announced that the tropical storm was veering toward us and had been upgraded to a hurricane called Allison—the first of the season, unexpectedly early. We would turn back to West End Island to seek safe harbor.

Nine-foot waves broke over the bow and halfway back to the stern as we raced our little boat for cover. We pitched in all directions, with forty-five-degree angles common. It seemed we would surely slide off that open deck and into the violent sea. For four long hours, our battered craft defied the storm, finally arriving again at the island.

Tom knew of a relatively sheltered berth at an abandoned marina. The hotel there had burned down years before, and the previously thriving resort was deserted and in ruins. Former gardens were covered with weeds and thick tropical brush. Once grand, the blackened hotel was a water-stained, roofless shell, half covered with vines. The scene was eerie, ghostly in the grey light.

After a warming shower and a stiff drink, I escaped the crowded boat during a brief lull in the rain. Strolling the rickety quay, I tried to make sense of my predicament. The burned hotel mirrored the wreckage of my former life back home—ruined and abandoned. Still, I was alive, safe for now from the roiling sea. Solid earth felt comforting, even on a sodden, deserted island. My mood lightened. I felt almost cheerful.

Monday morning, I began to awaken at 6:00. The constant throb of the generator seemed louder than before, and the boat was rocking a lot. I thought that the engines were running and that we were underway. Full of hope for dolphins, I sat up quietly to plan what I would need for the deck: my underwater camera, the new fins I bought in Freeport, and my dive skins to ward off "sea ants," jellyfish larvae that deliver itchy stings. All set. As I lurched into the passage, Liz, the cook, squeezed past and told me that we were still moored! The heavy rocking was from wave action *inside* the harbor.

A glum Captain Tom reported bad news at breakfast. "Hurricane Allison hit Florida yesterday and is crossing South Carolina now. It looks like it will curve back down to the Atlantic and straight toward us. We can't move from this pier today."

Time crawled through that empty day. People played cards, read, tried to find some dry spot to rest from the storm. Desperately bored, I asked myself why I chose this trip. Was I trying to prove my courage or my independence? Was it to discover that dolphins aren't subject to our feeble ambitions? Was it to battle long-standing claustrophobia in a bunk half the size of a coffin? Maybe I just had to prove to myself that I can survive both inner and outer tempests.

The storm raged on. Day after day came and passed slowly. Still stranded in the abandoned harbor, we dashed outside in moments of sunshine, then rushed back, drenched, when torrents of rain moved in again. Squall lines paraded across the water at the rate of one every hour or so, each as wild as the last. Dense rains looked like waterfalls as they approached, and the mighty surf shot pure white froth thirty feet in the air.

Nearing the end of our disappointing week, still tied to the pier at West End Island, I suffered emotional extremes: hope, despair, fear, regret, impatience, even occasional humor. The week presented a strange microcosm of life's reality. It was raw, without any guidebook.

Key to Acceptance

Hurricane Allison finally passed. We had only one day left on our dive boat before we were scheduled to end our trip. Wednesday's dawn brought calm waters, clear skies, and a white-hot sun. By 6:30, the *Sea Fever* sped toward the fabled shallow areas where dolphins might be found. Directly after breakfast, we gathered our snorkel gear and waited … and waited. Circling the areas where dolphins were "nearly always" sighted, we watched intently for three hours with no reward. The week's disappointment was unchanged.

Hours of boredom alternated with moments of adrenalin. It was exhausting to sit in the intense sun, surrounded by diesel fumes and deafening engine noise. We would see a dolphin or two, playing in our wake or running just in front of the bow. Each time we stopped, the dolphins would disappear.

Hours passed. We were losing hope of seeing a pod, when the dolphins found us! They came in small groups of three or four or five, running the bow, gliding only a foot or so in front of the boat, swimming exactly at our same speed. We greeted each sighting with cheers, hanging over the rails with cameras snapping. The dolphins were exquisitely graceful, gliding effortlessly in perfect formation. As before, though, when we got into the water, the shy creatures would dive. They seemed interested in playing with our boat but not with us. Again and again, hearing

Tom's urgent "Dive! Dive! Dive!" we were thwarted. Only once was I fast enough to get close. The dolphin danced there a moment, turned a graceful pirouette with its nose straight up, then swam away. It was a magnificent specimen, perhaps eight feet long. But so quickly gone! The sun finally set on a dejected group of hunters.

Late that night, sitting alone on the top deck, I watched flecks of moonlight dance on a calm sea. This journey did, after all, have its special moments. With gratitude, I examined my favorite mental snapshots: Floating on gentle waves that first day in Lucaya; brilliant colors of a spectacular sunset between pulses of the storm; powerful, towering surf, pounding massive rocks at West End. I pictured my Japanese cabin-mate, Amaya, shining in her yellow slicker, wading across a ten-foot puddle during a break in the winds. Elusive, teasing dolphins, gliding silently beside the *Sea Fever* bow will remain in memory. I will celebrate my one close encounter with a wild dolphin, brief and tantalizing. It is enough. Hurricane Allison taught me to overcome fear, to trust my own strength, moment by moment. So my stormy journey ended with acceptance. Wiser now, I could return to the ordinary magic of home.

A Wide World of Water

THE STINGRAYS ARE ALL AROUND ME, SWOOPING TO THE surface of the warm, turquoise water. One glides in front of me, skimming the waves with graceful, wing-like fins. Another comes even closer. I stroke its silky smooth back as it undulates by, inches from my shoulder. Easily treading the salty water, it feels perfectly natural to swim alongside such graceful, nonaggressive creatures. These gentle angels of Ambergris Caye seem simply curious, unafraid of human companions. Thrilled by their closeness, I feel no fear, only wonder and kinship.

I came to Belize with my longtime friends Linda and Michael, who invited me to vacation with their family shortly after my divorce. Still searching for a comfortable new identity, I was thrilled by the chance to explore the second-largest reef in the world, in the company of loyal allies. I also wanted to make up for my disappointing search for dolphins in the Bahamas.

For the first five days, we stayed at a remote hunting lodge in the tropical forest on the Belize mainland. While I found this jungle portion of the trip interesting, it was also intimidating and often uncomfortable. A roaring river in a chasm below our cabins reminded me of the wildness of the place. Swarms of black flies delivered painful stings. Sleeping alone in a large, rustic cabin, I woke to monkeys clambering over the shutters. I even shared my roofless shower with a family of pack rats.

After our stay at the lodge, we flew in a bush plane to Ambergris Caye. I was secretly relieved to trade the chatter of monkeys for the soothing breath of the surf. We arrived safely in San Pedro, the island's quaint fishing village, and settled into a modest beachfront resort. It was quiet and restful. No hurry here! Most endearing was the absence of cars. Everyone travels all over the island in golf carts. Six of us piled onto our one cart to bump merrily over rutted dirt roads.

The highlight of Ambergris Caye was swimming its azure waters in the company of giant rays. The natural world nourishes my soul, particularly in ocean or mountain settings where I feel entirely at home—at one with all life. I'm certain of our interconnection. All creatures of nature are equally precious. Swimming with stingrays was a spiritual experience for me. I felt overwhelming gratitude throughout our time at the reef. The graceful rays remain a precious memory.

From childhood, I've been drawn to bodies of water—oceans, rivers, and lakes. Our family cabin at Grand Lake o' the Cherokees was a summertime retreat from the time I was nine. Situated in northeast Oklahoma, the lake is nestled in the foothills of the Ozark Mountains. With thirteen hundred miles of shoreline, it is usually simply called Grand Lake. Our cabin was on the hill above an inlet named Duck Creek. I learned to swim in that protected cove, jumping fearlessly off the boat dock.

Indelible images of lighthearted weekends at the lake crowd my mind, even now. *Fishing for bass with Daddy in his little aluminum boat, guiding its outboard troll motor as he expertly cast his lure along the bank. Plunging into the cool lake to ease July's humid heat. Angling for crappie with my short rod and reel, bare feet dangling from the dock. Watching sunfish glint by, as they darted under the boat ramp. Setting off our own fireworks display at the top of the hill on the Fourth of July. Reading Laura Ingalls Wilder novels on the screened-in porch and napping away languid afternoons on the bunk beds there.*

For my Dad and his buddies who visited our place, fishing was the major attraction. His favorite lures had funny names—Hula-Popper, Lazy Ike. Once, we caught a catfish on the trotline that was so huge it fed the whole weekend crowd at a campfire fish fry. There were humorous moments too, like the time Dad's friend Walt, a little tipsy, called it a day. He headed for the cabin in the dark, but walked past the ramp and straight off the end of the dock. We pulled him out of the lake like a big fish, with much merriment about the "catch of the day." I carry such memories as the prized payload of a blissful childhood.

My affinity for expanses of water grew in adulthood to include oceans and rivers, discovered through a thirty-year history of world travel with Jim and more recent adventures with my second husband, Dale. Jim and I visited the Caribbean, Tahitian, Hawaiian, and Greek Islands, as well as many coastal villages of Mexico. We cruised the primitive Orinoco River where natives of remote Venezuela still traded with animal skins and beads. We rocked on a schooner through the northeast Caribbean around St. Martin, Antigua, Nevis, and St. Kitts. Memorably, we sailed the Grenadines from St. Vincent to Grenada in a sixty-five-foot ketch. After my second marriage to Dale, the two of us explored most of the major rivers of Europe, from Amsterdam to the Black Sea. For our honeymoon trip, we cruised around the horn of South America, traveling from Santiago, Chile, to Patagonia and the Falklands, ending in Buenos Aires, Argentina. On other adventures, we crossed the Atlantic by ship and later sailed the Inland Passage to Alaska. There is an obvious theme here: water!

During these and other seagoing adventures, I repeatedly plunged into the deep with unrealistic expectation, learning over time that ecstatic moments were serendipitous blessings, never to be taken for granted. They couldn't be forced or manufactured, even in promising settings. My disappointment in missing the dolphins after a storm's intervention is just one example. Hurricane Allison in the Bermuda Triangle changed everything about that particular trip but also taught its own unique lessons.

Another instance of such disappointment was an earlier attempt to swim with bottlenose dolphins. I was in the Florida Keys for my Watsu certification. The day after those training sessions ended, my friend Peggy and I visited the nearby Dolphin Research Center. We wanted to experience swimming with a pod of dolphins in the center's narrow cove, cordoned off from the open sea.

Once again, weather affected our outcome. The large sea mammals were in a crowded, closed space, not really a natural setting. A tropical storm had passed overnight, and the trapped dolphins were agitated. I believe they were oppressed by the manipulated situation at the Center. Though Peggy and I both were able to complete the "dorsal pull," holding a dolphin's dorsal fin to be pulled through the water as it swam, my dolphin became aggressive, and I had to leave the water quickly. That was a contrived, commercial experience that I regretted.

Disappointments like this are a likely consequence of arrogantly assuming that we can control nature. In reality, we fit into the natural environment as one of the countless creatures of the earth. We are neither above nor below them in importance. At best, we simply take our place among all living things, grateful participants in the divine Whole.

Finisterra

Where the Sea of Cortez
marries the Pacific,
melding waters on this Sunday shore,
foamy tide climbs to its higher shelf,
washes my bare legs,
erases footprints of earlier walkers.
A brilliant sun flexes muscles,
stronger here than in my mountain home.
This sensuous feast awakens every cell,
quickens my spirit to see
beyond mere eyes.

Walking to the point,
I admire precise herringbone patterns
drawn in the sand by the reaching tide.

Fluid fabric washes flat, then emerges again
as weaver waves retreat.
Abundant life! Shining out
like glints of sun dancing from here
to the flat line where sea meets sky.
This morning at daylight,
charter boats, armed with monster poles
to hook blue marlin,
paraded past this same beach,
converged at Cabo's pier
and swallowed macho warriors
who pay to kill.
Humbler fisher folk stand in the surf,
casting long lines
to reel in a writhing prize.
Mexican natives, simpler still,
work only with line, hook, and weight,
clinging with bare feet to high granite
at the far end of the beach
stalking Jack Crevalle for tonight's table.
Smaller dramas play out at my feet.
Tiny crabs dig instant dens
sucking sand behind them
in perfect round pits.
So many of them!
After a wave, the beach bubbles
like pudding in a pot,
pouring nutrients into blind mouths.

Another wave. Tiny mullet

wash up too far.
Stranded like driftwood,
wide eyes stare into space
as silver slivers flop and gasp
drowning in air.
Moved, I pick them up,
toss them back
to their wet haven,
breathe easier myself.
But two large crabs scuttle past
into the fringe of foam
taking breakfast.
Token rescues don't matter—
creatures live their karma
to feed waiting crabs or flocking vultures
or other appropriate predators.
This is a beach buffet for true natives
and always has been.
I walk more slowly toward the point,
pondering fate.
Twenty feet from shore,
a lone pelican performs
his death-defying dive
crashing like kamikaze
to gulp his breakfast prey.

The point looms now.
Finisterra, land's end,
end of the earth.

What dark beast waits
in shadows of rocks
or smiles in innocent sunlight
to feast on this flesh?
What ocean of wisdom
will take me
and to what end?

—*Cabo San Lucas*

Ever Green

ON A BRIGHT AUTUMN SUNDAY, I FELT RESTLESS AND confined indoors, so I shut down the computer, pulled on my jeans and hiking boots, and headed for the mountains. My favorite nearby hike is the Anne U. White trail north of Boulder. It was breezy and sixty degrees there. The light was pure clarity—that special, tentative, delicious sunlight that reaches your soul on a cloudless October day in Colorado. Fourmile Creek was dry that day, so I hopped like a cat over the rocks, as the trail crossed and re-crossed the creek bed.

Without analyzing it, I searched for a sign, some special message from nature. The voice of the Ultimate Mystery moves with the wind through these pine-tops. That wind was the only sound in the deep silence of the canyon. I reveled in the sunshine warming my back, feeling peaceful as I hiked alone. Pausing at the base of a low cliff, I imagined a lone cougar, perhaps lurking among rocks, watching me from his high perch. I looked, but no cat appeared.

Scrambling around a bend, I found my metaphor. Down in a draw, leaning over the creek bed, a piñon pine had bent down to the ground. Heavy snows in the bitter winter had nearly broken its back, but not quite! Bent, not broken, its needle fingertips touched the earth on the opposite bank. It must have bowed in this attitude of devotion for many months.

The miracle is that the tree didn't die. Though the trunk was scarred at the bend-point, the roots didn't die. Instead, limbs on the sun-side of the recumbent trunk had begun to grow, reaching up for the light. One leader branch emerged in last summer's warmth, startling in its beauty and strength. It was like a new tree—fresh!—rebirthed from the sound, healthy roots of its old life. It was a wonder that mirrored my own regeneration. With renewed energy, I climbed on to the top of the hill, then sang on the trail back down.

That day, I was surprised by joy. It welled up from the same earth that nurtured a fresh start in the tree—new today but grounded in the old. That moment, I felt young again, strong and buoyant and free. Bent, not broken. Alone, not lonely. Ever green.

The memorable image of the bowed tree is just one example of awareness emerging through nature. Unforeseen insights lie cloaked in ordinary experience. Who knows what epiphany may arise while canoeing, gardening, or hiking a mountain trail? Who can guess what new perception waits in tropical waters? An insight can even hide in a pile of raked leaves. Such "aha! moments" are best expressed in poetry, for poems distill meaning, like unexpected glints of light shining out from dark places. Writing down these flashes unlocks conscious awareness of untapped wisdom.

Autumn Light

Cleaning four-o'clock beds is a rite.
Summer's end, nod to autumn.
Crackling dry leaves fall together
with etched, mazelike designs
each unique in its scarred demise.
There is a brilliance in fall light.
Ideas come whole
like the last sweet raspberry
plucked by grimy gloves
from its sheltered place on the fence.
Aching poignancy of clear thought
burns with the flame of a maple.
Life is vibrant in autumn light:
bittersweet, understood,
and short.

Warwick Dawn

THE CHARTERED TOUR BUS BUMPED ALONG A NARROW country highway, bound for the welsh border west of Cheshire, England. Perched on the back seat of the bus, we watched wintry pastures roll by, their low stone fences far removed from the rush of London and smoky streets of Birmingham, our first two stops on a ten-day music and theater tour of England. Under low-hanging January clouds, rain-glazed fields hosted small herds of Holsteins, grazing peacefully as we passed. Our hospitable Welsh bus driver joked that these cattle in Wales are happier than English cows. "Notice how they smile. … They are laughing stock!" His cheery witticisms lightened the gray day.

January is not the best time to tour England, particularly during such a frigid winter as this. Everything seemed dark and shadowed. The first two days in London, I felt isolated and wretchedly cold. I did have a burst of emotional sunshine there, receiving confirmation that my divorce from Jim was final December 31. With the sale of our company also settled last fall, that shattering chapter has ended at last. It took almost four years to be free of my failed marriage, beset by complications, delays, and secrecy. After thirty-three years married, how does a new divorcée act? Who am I now? I thought this trip might offer some clues.

When I decided to come to England, I intended it as a personal reward, a celebration of the closure of my divorce from Jim. It would be a marker of new independence, hard-earned after those extra years of living together to hide his secret. Still, I felt some apprehension. I knew no one on the sponsoring university's list of participants. Would I be comfortable in the group? I thought of people I knew who might come along for company.

Back in September, I had an appointment downtown with Dale Meyer, a Chamber of Commerce comrade. The autumn sun was warm on our backs, as we sipped wine and enjoyed a quiet talk at a sidewalk café. We had known each other professionally for several years, occasionally meeting for lunch or coffee to discuss community projects. Each of us had chaired the Chamber Board and served terms on our respective boards. Dale is a behavioral economist and distinguished professor who regularly travels internationally to attend professional association meetings and do consulting. Would this educational tour interest him? With little hope that it would work, I enthusiastically described my planned trip, especially the segments in Wales and Cheshire and Warwick, places I had not visited before. When I next saw the tour's participant list, I was happy to see that Dale had signed up to go.

Our travel group gathered in London, where we celebrated New Year's Eve together at our hotel. The schedule was light during the next two days there. Many venues were closed for the holiday, so we were on our own much of the time. We ate pub food on New Year's Day in the only establishment we found open, and bought fruit at a small grocery near the hotel. Most of those free days, we walked, explored nearby parks, and talked of many things.

Dale and I were the only single people on this tour. Our companions were older, long-married retired couples, supporters of the university's music and theater programs. Without Dale, I would have sat alone at the back of the tour bus. I was glad that he came, though I recognized that he also felt hesitant. He wasn't sure how to be with me, given our years of arms-length professional involvement in the public eye. During our Chamber years, while I was actively promoting my business, he helped initiate the Center for Entrepreneurship at CU, becoming a celebrated pioneer in that academic field. Our previous friendship was entirely professional, but this trip challenged that defined level. It was liberating and promising, but also a little scary.

With the holiday past, our whole group met for a bus tour of London and a visit to Shakespeare's Globe Theatre site. After the day-long organized sightseeing, Dale and I got away for an intimate dinner at one of London's finest restaurants. Our conversations over the weekend had gone far beyond superficial topics to reveal our dreams and fears. Far away from CU and the Boulder Chamber and my all-business persona, I marked that night as my fresh start as a single woman. But the next day, I felt awkward and strange. I didn't know quite how to relate. I was so terribly out of practice at "dating." My God, I was more than fifty years old and was married to the same man for most of my life!

Despite my uncertainties, Dale and I continued our private conversations as we rode the tour bus to Birmingham to attend a concert by their rightfully famous symphony orchestra. Our group spent only one night in Birmingham, then traveled to North Wales the following day to sample its pastoral countryside and tour a slate mine near the border. Dale was particularly thoughtful on that drive. He was mostly quiet, staring intently into the darkening landscape surrounding the bus.

"Are you upset about something?" I asked.

"I'm thinking about slate mines and remembering my childhood in Mingo Junction. It was a grimy mill town on the Ohio River. Most of the workers emigrated from places like this—from the mines and farms and factories of Wales and Ireland and Hungary and Italy."

His voice softened. "They came to America to escape hopeless drudgery, only to get stuck in that hellish steel mill."

This cold, shadowed landscape opened a storehouse of dark memories for Dale. We rode quietly for a time. His silence gave me a glimpse of long-standing sadness. Arriving at the mine, the bus turned onto a dirt road, passing mountainous piles of steel-gray slate, broken in flat, thin pieces. The slate was only slightly darker gray than the lowering clouds. The dim landscape, devoid of color and light was depressing.

I watched Dale's pensive face, surprised by his honesty. He was trusting me with the harshness of his childhood, offering insight into the man he became. Neglect and deprivation motivated his compulsion to achieve, his workaholic drive to win layers of professional recognition. Like me, he's had to prove his strength—if only to himself.

Arriving at the mine, we filed out of the bus to stretch out the kinks from our long ride. There wasn't much there: A small shop and bar, heaps of slate, narrow tracks for the ore cars that rumble into the bowels of the mine. Peering down into that black hole, I was daunted by claustrophobia. The mine tunnel looked so cramped that people might bump their heads riding through. How could I breathe down there? In a wave of dread, I elected to stay above ground, while all the others climbed into modified ore cars and slid into the dark.

Sitting with a glass of wine in the deserted bar adjoining the gift shop, I waited for the tour to return. I thought about these bleak surroundings and what I had learned about Dr. Dale. I wondered about his impressions and memories, down there in the depths of the earth. Even more deeply, I marveled at the courage—or desperation—of the generations of men and young boys who labored in mines like this one. It sapped their spirit. It's no surprise that the suicide rate here is still extraordinary.

Over our few days in England, Dale and I had already shared many experiences of our early years and our work. He spoke of his childhood poverty and the people who enabled his improbable rise to the life of a respected academic. He received a superior education at Northwestern University on a fully paid scholarship, scrabbling together his livelihood as a busboy, a cab driver, and whatever other work he could manage along with school. With a Danforth Fellowship, he finished his PhD in Iowa and spent most of his award-winning teaching career in Colorado. Dale's vulnerability in speaking of his lonely childhood and lack of familial affection made me want to ease his deprivation.

When he emerged from the mine, Dale's melancholy had deepened. I felt raw and wounded on his behalf. As our bus pulled away from the mine, finally rolling toward Chester, I squeezed his hand in empathy.

Chester was a luminous place, far removed from the dark slate mine, but my excitement was dimmed by the thought that Dale had to leave the tour early. He was scheduled to fly to Atlanta to attend a board meeting of the International Council of Small Business. With our growing connection, I dreaded his leaving. Was I simply lonely and sentimental, or could I be falling in love? Either way, I wanted to make every minute count in this fabled Old World city, a place that neither of us had explored before.

Built by the River Dee, near the border with Wales, Chester was founded as a Roman fort in 79 AD, one of the three main Roman army camps in Britannia. The original walls around the city were later strengthened and extended by the Saxons. Some of these walls still remain, with a footpath running along the top. The streets are lined with medieval buildings, their white and black facades preserved later by Victorian restoration. The path on top of the wall near Eastgate afforded our best views of the town. We strolled along, looking down at the shops and dwellings, marveling at the sense of antiquity. Everything seemed authentic, nothing like artificial replicas in a Hollywood set. The whole town looked like an illustration for a British history textbook.

We spent most of the day on our own to explore this enchanting place. We visited the town hall and the cathedral, a Gothic Revival structure that dates back to the Norman era. I snapped my own pictures of the most photographed clock in England (after Big Ben), high on the Eastgate Tower. Our favorite section was The Rows, in central Chester, unique in Britain. Those streets were lined with the town's signature medieval architecture.

Some shops on the ground floor were lower than the street level, entered by steps leading to crypt-like vaults. At the entrance to one of these buildings, Dale stopped to read a posted menu. He was well practiced at finding outstanding restaurants, the result of years of living alone and mostly eating out.

"This looks really interesting. This structure was built on top of Roman ruins. The restaurant is down below, within those ancient walls."

Intrigued, we gingerly descended worn stone steps into a candlelit dining room, set with white tablecloths and gleaming silver. Breathing in the history of this unique place, we were shown to a table for two, made private by a low, broken stone wall. Resting there after our long day of walking, savoring elegant food and quiet conversation, sharing good cabernet, I felt completely at ease with this sensitive man.

Our travel companions were curious about where we'd been all day, as we slipped into the concert hall for our last musical program in Chester. Dale's flight to Atlanta was scheduled out of Heathrow Airport for the following day. He would leave Chester at daylight to make his flight, and our tour would drive later to Stratford for four more days of sight-seeing. I dreaded climbing on the bus alone.

As Dale and I reluctantly said goodnight after the concert, he held me close in a long hug. I went into my room with another sense of loss. A midnight knock on my hotel door set my heart racing. I knew it was Dale.

"I couldn't leave without seeing you again," he whispered. I opened the door wide. This was our real beginning, a new dawn of sincere love.

Warwick Dawn

Icy English half-moon's
translucent tender light
slips into lacy fog
soft on the cheek of dawn.
Colors kiss these wintry eyes—
Tudor rose, edged in gold
turns gray to lighter pink
in virgin folds of clinging cloud.
Held close and safe
until the night,
Moon's shyness relents,
welcomes the embrace
of Warwick's morning fog.
How can I say what I feel?
Transforming pain to hope
this glow begins a clearer day.

Watsu: Spiritual Therapy

THE ABRUPTNESS OF JIM'S COMING OUT TRANSFORMED MY outer life and presented a recurring puzzle: who am I now? I suffered from career withdrawal. My identity confusion continued for several years and prompted ever-deeper personal exploration. One of those ventures was becoming a certified watsu practitioner. Water shiatsu techniques offered unexpected spiritual satisfaction and a pat answer to the frequent, dreaded question, "What are you doing now?" Earning certification to practice this warm-water therapy became an important element of a fresh self-image.

My first watsu experience was amazingly powerful. I entered the Mapleton Hospital therapy pool, hopeful that the treatment might relax my sore neck muscles, chronically tightened by stress. I knew almost nothing about this technique, which my massage therapist had recommended. With roots in zen shiatsu, watsu is a federally registered service mark used to describe a method of water massage developed in california by harold dull. Technically, it is a muscle reeducation approach involving gentle mobilization of joints and soft tissue while immersed in warm water.

I immediately liked the practitioner, Peggy Schoedinger, a highly respected professional physical therapist with more than sixteen years of experience at the hospital and in private practice. She was also a Watsu specialist and instructor. We entered the pool, welcomed by comforting warmth. With my back against the pool wall, my feet firmly planted, and my arms floating comfortably, Peggy instructed me to close my eyes and relax, assuring me that she would support my head throughout the session. I should just let go. I did exactly that and soon felt my body moving through the water, gently stretched and always supported.

How does it feel to be sea grass, wafted to and fro by gentle currents, gracefully swaying with the rhythm of ocean waves? During this first Watsu experience, I became that sea grass in my mind. At times, we moved rapidly; then we would slow to stillness. The pace changed frequently, but always with a peace-ful grace. I was held safely, first drifting like seaweed in the warm water, then feeling my back gently pushed in undulating waves. My muscles were tenderly stretched, my tension easing as I relaxed into the experience. Eyes closed, I was enfolded like a child, then released to float, free of restraint and all responsibility.

Too soon, I again felt my back leaned against the pool wall, my feet gently planted. I opened my eyes to see Peggy's soft smile and Namaste bow. I wanted to weep for joy. I felt deeply peaceful, utterly relieved of tension. My body felt taller, loose, relaxed, yet oddly stimulated. I later said that I could "feel all my cells." It seemed like a tender rebirth—no expectations, no prescriptions, no preconceived outcomes.

A Calling

Watsu was such a divine gift, I was filled with a desire to share it with others. In the weeks that followed, I read about Watsu and learned that it is not some esoteric gimmick with questionable benefit. It is used throughout the world in hospitals and clinics, as well as in luxurious spas. The Worldwide Aquatic Bodywork Association (WABA) promotes it, but professional medical therapists, like Peggy, use it to ease symptoms of stroke, multiple sclerosis, traumatic injury, substance abuse, and other conditions.

After my investigation of the technique, I shared with Peggy my aspiration to become a certified Watsu practitioner. The timing was perfect. An intensive training was scheduled in Florida the next month, and she was one of four instructors. It was my chance to learn from the best how to share this treasure as a certified practitioner.

In May 1998, I flew to Marathon in the Florida Keys. Our training would take place in a sweet, quiet setting at an aging resort on the beach. Their large, shallow swimming pool was ideal for Watsu practice in chest-deep water. We had an intense schedule of work: three water sessions a day, two dry land classes, and personal study time during the heat of the day. We met at the pool at 7:30 a.m. and continued nonstop until 9:30 or 10:00 at night. While our schedule was tight and relentless, the work was enjoyable, particularly as the "receiver" of Watsu treatments, as students practiced on each other. Each day seemed three days long because of its segmentation, and I forgot any thought of restful leisure. It was a change of pace and scene but definitely not a vacation.

Our teachers explained carefully and articulately each move in the water. Their demonstrations were beautiful ballets; our student repetitions felt awkward in contrast. We began with the most basic patterns of movement, which also punctuate divisions between more complex segments of the basic Watsu flow. We practiced critical transitional moves and thought about how to pace our work to meet the needs of individual clients.

Watsu techniques have esoteric names: rotating accordion, head capture, arm-leg rock, seaweed, thread the needle, far leg over, sacrum pull, undulating spine, fin pull, open saddle, Hara rock. Each one requires a whole series of precise moves, leading into another whole series of precise moves. After a couple of days, my mind was boggled and my confidence shaken. How can Peggy make this look effortless, her face the picture of compassion, as she constantly monitors her receiver?

It was hard. Everything that looks so simple from the pool deck seems incredibly difficult when a limp person is in your arms and you are the engine that makes the Watsu system run. As days passed, my feet were blistered, back muscles stressed, upper body strength challenged. Each night, my fifty-eight-year-old body was exhausted, skin ravaged by sun and chlorine. Once, I completely fell apart, clinging to the side of the pool and crying like a child. Peggy helped me realize that this was a normal reaction to fatigue. I kept going.

During the weeks of class, time stopped. There was only the schedule: water, study, class, water, class, water—with precious breaks to rest from the sun and humidity, study, eat and sleep.

We practiced and practiced and then visualized the sequences and transitions in our minds. We ate and slept Watsu. We talked about it and watched training videos, then practiced some more. Every motion has a purpose; every technique preplanned and intentional, though the receiver is blissfully unaware of any of this. The receiver simply relaxes and drifts effortlessly through crystal water, letting care and tension wash away.

All of us dreaded the final exam, when we would demonstrate the whole Watsu sequence on strangers, under watchful eyes of the four instructors. I wondered who might be assigned to me as a "model," the recipient of my demonstration. Man or woman? Tall or short, heavy or slim? Knowledgeable or naïve about this type of bodywork? I wouldn't know until 7:30 Monday morning, when my test was scheduled.

The Test

I woke at 5:30 on Monday morning. Unable to relax, I thought about all the Watsu moves, visualizing each transition. Lights on, I studied my notes, laid aside only five hours before. I felt more confident when the alarm went off an hour later. Still nervous, I made tea and ate applesauce to settle my stomach. Tests never bothered me before, but they were all language-based. This is different! This time, I must dance through the water with a partner who could be ill, neurotic, healthy, old, athletic, young, or even pregnant. I thought through the transitions again and again, practicing in my mind.

7:20 a.m., pool-side. Still nervous, I received the intake form for my model. She was a woman named Becca, telemarketer, northern Florida resident, no experience with Watsu. (Good— no preconceptions about the techniques. She won't know if I goof.) However, she was also a former massage student, with an interest in reiki. Not so naïve. Then I read the preconditions section of the form. To my dismay, Becca had all kinds of physical limitations. Stiff neck, slipped disc (several years ago), prone to dislocation in the hip. Worse, she was susceptible to motion sickness. A Watsu nightmare is having the client get seasick!

Flashing through the sequence of moves, I realized that my worry about getting this client's leg over my shoulder and the other leg around my waist was unnecessary. No fin pulls for this gal! I couldn't perform any of those flexing tricks! She was able to receive only the most basic moves. Hoping that she wouldn't be bored, I began. Tense, my stiffness transferred into Becca's neck and back and facial muscles. Her head was rigid in the crook of my arm.

After a quarter-hour of worrying about "what's next," feeling self-conscious because all four instructors watched me skip move after move that might hurt Becca, I finally settled into the real purpose of the session: making the *receiver* feel relaxed, renewed, and refreshed. Concentrating on this special person instead of my own insecurities, I noticed how vulnerable Becca was, trusting me to support her in the water. I was filled with a motherly tenderness toward this unique being floating in my arms. Kindness warmed my heart and I began to release my own tension. Almost immediately, Becca's face softened into a slight smile, the wrinkles around her eyes relaxed, her head became heavy and loose, and her whole body moved with the steady rhythm of her breath and the calming motion of the water. After an hour of simply moving together through the water, feeling present in each moment, we finally returned to the pool wall and completed the session. Becca's face glowed with contentment. After a smiling moment, she said, "May I hug you?" And she did.

Compassion in Action

Later, I got it: when my focus shifted from myself to Becca, the whole session transformed from a conceptual challenge to a manifestation of human compassion. I was taking good care of another person. When I could simply be with her, Becca relaxed as well and became deeply tranquil. Trust was established, and she benefitted as much from my healing intention as from the Watsu technique. My work in the water became compassion in action.

During our evening debriefing, many others expressed similar thoughts. Miriam spoke of her nervousness and confessed that she completely froze when she began her session. She forgot everything and panicked for a moment. Then she thought, "This receiver can be *my* teacher," and she relaxed a little. "Then the water took over and I was able to stop thinking," she said. From then on, everything was fine. Darcy summed it up: "When you think too much, you stall." Harold Dull, Watsu's originator, taught that this re-bonding therapy is as healing for the giver as for the person being floated. "The more we feel our oneness with others, the freer we can be in ourselves," he says in one training video.

I have always loved being in and near water. It refreshes my spirit. My first treatment with Peggy opened the door into a completely different calling, and I practiced Watsu semi-professionally for several years afterward. I had heartfelt engagement with those I treated, and their appreciation was genuine. "I felt much lighter," said one, calling her experience a "primal vacation," praising "the nurturing effect from the combination of water and gentleness of treatment." Another recalled "rushes of joy and a sense of being in a waking dream." Unlike conventional massage, the water itself works this magic.

Back in my home pool, offering Watsu to my clients in quiet privacy, my broken self-confidence began to mend. I regained trust and general awareness of my own body's strength. Spiritually, it opened a way to exchange self for other in compassionate healing. Through this service, my own soul was restored.

Journey to the Source

THE WALLS OF THIS CANYON ARE NEARLY WHITE. WITH no pollution to soil the air or cloud the view, the azure sky is nearly blinding. Even as clouds roll in, these canyon walls seem to shine above the chattering Yampa River. After last night's rain, the rocky ground is wet and cold this morning. Two days into my first canoe trip as a single woman, I breathe in the fragrant dampness like a tonic. In early morning light, the wide, tree-filled meadow where we're camped is resplendent with waving grass and yarrow and unfamiliar, delicate wild flowers. A small mesa, rising to the east, is dotted with mesquite and sage. A quick brown movement makes me catch my breath. A lone fox trots to the river's edge for a morning drink. Suddenly startled, she disappears into the tall grass.

Last night, I pitched my one-person tent without help—yet another new experience. The rain soothed me into exhausted sleep, after battling fierce headwinds all afternoon. Those winds challenged even the most skilled canoeists. As a nervous novice, I thought my paddling partner and I were bound to dump, though we somehow managed to stay afloat. One canoe got stranded sideways on a boulder mid-river. It teetered there for breathless minutes. Powerless to help, we watched from a safer spot beyond the rapids, hooting encouragement as the frail-looking craft bumped around the hazard and finally turned downstream.

Those few hours yesterday were perilous. One canoe fell far behind when the two paddlers stopped to rest. We worried that they were in serious trouble until they finally came into camp at dusk. By the time everyone was accounted for and dinner was made, we were all ready to collapse. This first day was a test of endurance, especially for newcomers like me.

Why do I want to be here, knowing little about canoeing or primitive camping? Along with seventeen strangers in nine canoes, I paddle hard, carry heavy equipment to and from the canoe, set up my tent, and help cook. I sleep on the ground and shiver from the cold. It is hardly restful. But I feel alive! I'm free and natural here. This weekend trip marks a conscious break from my dependence on Jim and ordinary city existence. I am learning to be single, and I feel empowered.

This is a women's trip, dubbed Journey to the Source. Led by my psychologist friend, Deborah, we are exploring our spiritual connections with the natural world and looking for deeper meanings. Ben, our guide from the outfitter, is the only male here. A sensitive writer and teacher himself, he complements the group amazingly well. This morning, he was up before daylight to meditate, sitting cross-legged beside his tent. With years of experience guiding river trips each summer, his wilderness skills are outstanding, and his competent presence gives me more confidence.

Ben offered a lesson last night that tested our preconceptions and courage. When he went to his tent before dinner, he rummaged in his dry sack looking for a jacket. Instead, he found there a three-foot snake. He picked it up just behind its head and held it high for all of us to see. To me, it looked like a rattlesnake, with light brown and buff diamonds on its back, but it had no rattles. Ben assured us it was not poisonous. He gently passed the snake to braver souls and showed them how to hold it. It wrapped its body around wrists and hands, like a python. It was a big step for me just to touch the writhing creature, but Deborah fearlessly held it. She quipped that it made a "half-hitch" knot on her arm. Amazingly, the snake didn't seem afraid, and neither were we. We were simply curious. Deborah used the experience to exemplify our intrinsic connection with all living things.

After supper, we circled the campfire and talked of our day's adventures on the river. Without light pollution, the stars were brilliant. Only the fire gave more light. We dreamily watched it flare its varied golds, oranges, and blues. After Deborah led a simple meditation, we listened to her beat a perfect measure on her Native American "journey drum." The river sound accompanied this rhythm for reflection. Finally, we chanted a song as old as the tribes, filling me with indescribable peace.

> *Oh, Great Spirit,*
> *Earth, Sun, Sky and Sea,*
> *You are within*
> *And all around me.*

Though it was late, we wanted to hold onto these special moments. As usual, I sat a little apart from the others, very straight on the end of a fallen tree. Ben walked around behind me and silently, so gently, massaged my neck. My habitual storehouse of tension, those muscles are usually tight and sore. That compassionate gesture was a surprise. After a few moments, he lightly stroked the top of my head. It was a genuine act of kindness.

This morning dawned clear and calm. No major hazards are expected over the next few miles on the river. With my muscles sore from paddling against yesterday's wind, it is a pleasure to relax and let the current carry us. After lunch, we hold the silence, "returning to the source." No jokes, laughter, or human conversation interrupt our reverie, as we effortlessly guide our canoes downriver. The only sounds are lapping water and birdsong.

This remote, pristine river carved deep sandstone chasms in which thousands of canyon wrens live in mud nests that resemble bee hives. They are small birds with a bright white throat and chestnut breast. Their quick, angular flight leaves me breathless. At dawn this morning, I was roused by their clear, descending trill. Now, during our time of silent paddling, their flute-like call is as refreshing as the river.

Inspiring blue sky, puffs of summer cumulus clouds, and a light breeze keep us comfortable. The sandstone cliffs on this stretch are highlighted by fragrant sage and mesquite. I memorize the beauty of occasional verdant meadows, sliding past the bow of my canoe. A doe, drawn to the cold water for a drink, bolts as we round a sharp bend. Our world moves in slow motion. I embrace pure peace.

Still in silence, Ben motions us into our final evening camp-site. For tonight's campfire meditation, we are to bring a symbol of ourselves to share with the group. I take the poem I wrote the first night of our trip.

You can't see me …
I am the wind.
Gentle, calm, caressing, quiet,
elusive and playful
I stir the river for art and fun.

Changeable, exciting,
agitated, stormy,
moving darkness and lightning
across the horizon.

Rainbow riding,
I mix fear with beauty,
angry, destructive, then quiet,
submissive to the warming sun.
I dance with the grass
stir waves as I pass,
kiss each flower
to greet the spring.

Never the same,
always the same.
I am the wind, and (tonight)
I am at peace.

Awake in my sleeping bag this final night, wordless images of the river rush through my mind like a silent movie. These few days have opened fresh awareness and honed new skills. I learned to paddle effectively in the bow, while my canoe partner steered from the stern. Feeling competent and comfortable on the river is symbolic of other growth: Touching a snake without fear, trusting the kinship of new friends, cherishing the peace of silence, and finding inspiration in the canyon wren's song. I know the simmering joy of meditation alone on a high cliff, transformed by the sparkling view of the river below. I really *see* the incredible beauty of each tiny natural wonder: warm earth colors of lichens, rugged shapes of cliffs, sighs of the wind, the wrens' angular flight, natural perfection even in the skull of a rattlesnake, long dead. On this river, I'm at one with all of it, fearless. In my Journey to the Source, I've touched the power of the earth and found it also in myself.

Canyon Wren Prayer

Gushing cadence
trills down the scale.
Clear curved notes
carve silver songs
to wash red canyon walls.
Tawny tenor of desert cliffs,
sing again to bless these stones
open this tired heart
soften edges
waken new life.
Oh rusty wren,
raise your pure voice
speak for this pilgrim.
Sing thanks

for wild river roar
still evening peace.
Sing thanks.

Green River Hubris

D EB'S RELIABLE SUBARU IS SURE-FOOTED ON I-70, HUM-
ming through scattered showers on our way to Utah. It
is packed to the roof with gear for a canoe trip more demanding than the others I've experienced. After seven summers of
joining groups with competent outfitters providing equipment,
I'm set for my first unguided adventure. We are headed for a
four-day trip alone on Utah's Green River to christen Deborah's
brand-new canoe.

We're pushing the season a bit, this first week in May, but
the weather forecast shows possibility for relative comfort. We
watch the sky and point out "sucker holes," ephemeral patches of
blue opening in prevailing grey clouds. The changeable conditions remind me of a fragment of one of my poems:

> *Motoring across mountains,*
> *four seasons in an afternoon's journey:*
> *spring, then winter, then autumn gold,*
> *with summer our hope for tomorrow.*
> *Tentative rays through rain-veils*
> *drive us faster to our river.*
> *That river runs in my blood,*
> *a journey to the Source.*

Deb and I both have something to prove on this trip. Her forest-green canoe, a fifteen-foot Dagger Reflection, was a farewell gift from her former fiancé, perhaps to assuage his guilt for abruptly breaking off their engagement. Like me, she is trying to heal her wounded heart by taking this daring trip. We're both determined to test our strength and independence.

Packing her car was our first challenge this morning. Deb brought the basic camping equipment; I was in charge of the tent and our food. It was fun to plan menus, making meticulous lists of everything we would need for nourishing meals, including a box of wine to wash them down. I was ready when Deb arrived at daylight, everything stacked together in the corner of my study. We made several trips to the driveway and somehow found room for it all.

Eight scenic hours later, we check into The Mayor's House, a bed and breakfast near downtown Moab. The owner, actually a former mayor of the city, seems dubious about our planned adventure, looking skeptically at our loaded car when he greets us. Later, as we feast on Utah trout at the nearby Slick Rock Café, we laugh about the mayor's obvious doubts.

After a restless night, we stuff ourselves with the mayor's blueberry pancakes before our shuttle driver arrives. Deb knew just how to arrange for this young intern from the local wilderness school to shuttle our car to our take-out at Mineral Bottom. We follow Mike's yellow 1971 VW van over incredibly steep, narrow, muddy zig-zag ruts snaking down a fifteen-hundred-foot canyon wall. There is no rail, no shoulder, no margin for error. Mike races his rattling van down; we inch down behind him. At the bottom of the canyon, we park by the wide, flat river, near three or four other canoeists' cars.

We tie Deb's canoe to the top of Mike's van and start to transfer our gear. It's then that we make a dreadful discovery. I left our tent at home! I remember leaning it in the corner of my office, behind everything else I'd packed. In our hurry to leave, we somehow missed it. Too late for any remedy, we'll have to improvise a plastic fly as shelter.

On the dusty ride back up the canyon, Mike confides that he lived in this van for four years but now has a "stationary" home. He's a nice kid with clean energy. His confidence in his innate resourcefulness is encouraging to me, chastened by my mindless mistake in leaving the tent behind. With Deb's car located where we'll end our river route, Mike's van somehow climbs back up the canyon wall and clatters over a deserted two-lane road toward our put-in at Crystal Geyser. He helps us unload our gear and secure the canoe at river's edge, and we send him off with brave smiles and enthusiastic thanks.

As we tie in our gear, Deborah tells me about this place, Crystal Geyser. It is actually a cold artesian well under the riverbed that periodically shoots water straight up nearly forty feet, sometimes twelve or fourteen hours a day. It looks something like Yellowstone geysers, with the same Sulphur smell, but there is no heat. Three or four "boiling pots" surround it, and minerals coat nearby slick rock with a rusty gold veneer. This natural "faucet" flows directly into the Green River. It's a wonder of nature.

Deborah studies her detailed geologic maps while we lunch on cheese, nuts, fruit, and apple juice. She's scouting possible camping sites for tonight. Two or three canoes pass us as we eat. Otherwise, we're completely alone in a primal realm of sandstone and river.

The wind has come up by the time we put into the Green. With rain predicted now for the weekend, I'm a bit apprehensive. The river is wide, the current strong and tricky. Muddy and thick, it swirls in frequent eddies. Though there is no whitewater here, we feel the current rushing under the canoe. We paddle in wind until 4:00, about twelve miles downriver, stopping at the first promising camping spot we see. It has been a long, hard, day, with little sleep last night in Moab.

While Deb sets up the noisy, flapping fly for our shelter, I make dinner. Gusts of wind deposit grit in any open container. I shield our salad by working with hands inside a plastic bag. Everything takes longer than usual, but we feel better after fortifying ourselves with the salad and pita pockets with spinach and blue cheese. In the dusky last light, I walk the hillside and find a couple of pretty pieces of quartz for my rock garden at home. As we settle down in near darkness, I discover another careless oversight. My flashlight is failing already, with no extra batteries. We have only one good light between us.

Erratic wind rattles our plastic fly through the night. There is no shelter on this hill from trees or shrubs. The rocky terrain is rather barren, with only sagebrush and low scrub pines. After some fitful sleep, Saturday morning dawns a bit clearer and definitely warmer. We cook our eggs on the one-burner camp stove, shielded by a makeshift barrier against intermittent gusts. Still, it's a lovely, warm morning, and we feel more cheerful once we're on the river. By hugging the bank, we manage to avoid some of the wind, still taking advantage of the strongest current.

In late afternoon, we come upon a likely camping spot that offers panoramic views in both directions. The river curves just beyond our camp into a huge U. We are in the twisting

Labyrinth Canyon, with thousand-foot sandstone walls and an island in the wide river just across from our campsite. A natural path leads from the river to an enormous amphitheater that faces three converging canyons. It would offer terrific hiking if we had more time. We take a quiet hour to rest and read and memorize the scene, colors changing in the waning light.

This campsite is on a flat spot, perfect for our fly shelter, surrounded on three sides with scrub oak. It's fairly protected from the rain that comes once again, right after we finish supper. We stow our hastily cleaned utensils and get into our sleeping bags, surrounded by our gear, staying fairly dry under the edges of the fly. Our exhausted sleep is interrupted around 2:00 by some large animal pushing through the brush right above our heads. We noticed deer scat earlier, but this would be a nocturnal animal, hunting. We sense its threatening presence, very close by. We hold our breath and wait, hoping it's only a deer. Finally, whatever it is, the creature moves on. The night is quiet again.

Sunday, our third day out, the river is running very fast and flat. It has risen considerably overnight. We break camp, repack, and push off around 9:30 in cold, gusty wind. After a couple of hours of difficult paddling, we tie the canoe to a tree, climb up a steep bank, and shelter ourselves under a rock ledge. Canned chicken sandwiches and tangerines cheer us up, as we study our map to spot our next overnight camp possibility. Deborah likes a place called Hey Joe, an abandoned mining camp frequented by canoe groups. There, we can expect good tent sites and hiking opportunities. The map also shows an old mining road, leading from Hey Joe all the way to Mineral Bottom, where Deb's car is parked. She quips, "We could even walk out from there," and we smile at the joke. It'll be much easier to paddle!

By late afternoon, we arrive at Hey Joe, where we find three canoes already beached. We first passed this family group a couple of days ago and exchanged friendly waves. This early in the canoe season, it is rare to see anyone at all. Green River is practically deserted in early May. We guess that their group will claim this great campsite, and we'll need to find another spot further down. Deb pulls out her maps to look again at other possibilities.

After just a few minutes, we see the other travelers returning to their canoes. Deborah greets them warmly, and I see a good example of river courtesy, as she chats with the patriarch of the family. We're relieved to learn that they've only stopped briefly to explore the mine and are going several miles further to spend the night at Spring Canyon. As her conversation unfolds, Deb suddenly realizes that she already knows these people. Fifteen years ago, she worked at the same wilderness school as the bearded father, and she took his daughter on a camping trip near Steamboat. The girl, now a young wife, is here with her husband on their family trip. She is thrilled to see Deb again in this unlikely coincidence. After a bit of reminiscing, the group pushes off to paddle on their way.

As soon as their canoes disappear around the next bend, we pull our craft high onto a sheltered sand bar to unload. An excellent flat, sandy tent site is just a few feet away. This is the best campsite of our trip! It's near the river, but on top of a steep, four-foot bank above the water. It's sheltered completely by gnarly tamarisks, somewhat protected from wind and rain. Many previous campers have already carved out a cozy enclave for our rain fly.

With about half of our gear unloaded beside the canoe, we decide to carry some things up onto the higher bank. Deb returns for another load. Suddenly I hear her scream. Our canoe is loose, floating away!

A sudden surge of the swollen river lifted the lightened canoe off the sand bar. I race to the bank and see it swirling past in fast current. Deb grabs a life jacket and jumps in to swim for it. Both disappear around the bend. In a panic, I try to run along the edge of the river, thrashing around in thick brush, stumbling in the dense undergrowth. The tamarisks are taller than my head and I can't see anything! I run to the old mine and climb to the top of the shaft, trying to see beyond the brush, but the river is too far away, completely hidden by dense vegetation.

"What can I do?" I walk slowly back to the camp site, my feet feeling like wood. I try to gather courage, to breathe and find my calm center. My friend may be drowned. She couldn't possibly swim fast enough to catch the light canoe, floating on strong current. I'm not even certain that she got the life jacket on before she jumped in. If Deb did manage to save herself, she is probably on the other side of the river, too far down to come back. She has no food or water, unless she miraculously caught her canoe. It's late. No one else will be on the river tonight. What a dilemma!

I'm really alone now. Enervated and shaking with fear, I sit down on the edge of the river at our campsite, hope fading that another paddler might happen by. I quell panic by meditating. I pray that Deb is alive, safe. "Still the mind. Come back to the breath. Come back to the breath."

Soon it will be dark. I have to assess my resources—the few things we unloaded before we lost the canoe. I have two gallons of potable water, the rain fly, Deb's sleeping bag, and her dry bag with her clothes. I have my little day pack, our dry box with crackers and a few bread sticks, granola, and one small carton of soy milk. Useless now, Deborah's new wooden canoe paddle is here, along with my life vest. The canoe carried away my dry bag with all my clothes, my billfold and ID, and my sleeping bag, as well as all of our fresh food and most of the drinking water.

Dejected, I survey the pile of what is left, trying to decide what to do next, when I hear noises behind me. Another wild animal? I catch my breath when I turn and see a battered, wet, cold, sad Deborah stumble into the clearing. She's alive! She made it back, against all odds. I hug her with pure joy. She gave up hope of capturing the canoe and had to work hard to get herself out of the river and find her way back here. I'm overjoyed that she survived at all. She gets into some of her dry clothes, and we collapse on the river bank for another hour to watch futilely for passing boats. With any luck, some other group downriver will catch her unmanned craft and tow it to Mineral Bottom, or wherever they end their trip.

With darkness imminent, we set up a crude camp, just as it begins to rain again. Now that my friend is safely back, something odd happens to my body. I had held myself together through our immediate crisis, but now that it's over, I begin to shake uncontrollably, as if I were freezing cold. It's a delayed panic attack, and I'm helpless in its grip. Deb wraps me in her sleeping bag and has me drink some water. I feel weak and ashamed. She is the one who nearly died, yet she's taking care of me! Eventually, my shaking subsides, and Deb huddles into a makeshift sleeping bag rigged from her dry bag and a solar blanket, her head wrapped in an extra shirt. Too tired not to sleep, we take a little rest, wondering what the new day will bring.

At 5:00 a.m., the alarm on my wristwatch beeps. It's still too dark to see much, though we still have one working flashlight. I'm scared, but we do have a plan. We pack our absolute necessities in Deborah's small backpack and my fanny pack—first aid and extra shirts. We have no shoes, other than our Teva river sandals, but we have socks to pad our feet a little. We rig another pack out of Deb's dry bag to carry our water container. We're taking all the water we have, concerned about the dry hike ahead. We have to leave everything else behind at the campsite. Deborah writes a brief note, explaining our predicament, along with her home phone number. She requests the return of our gear, hoping someone will find it and carry it out. Before we leave, we share some granola and the little box of soy milk. We begin our walk at first light.

Remembering Deb's offhand remark that "we could walk out from here," we take the old mining road that leads to Mineral Bottom, *twenty-four miles away.* However, if we hurry, we might reach Spring Canyon before that family group leaves. If they can't take us along, they could at least send help when they reach Mineral Bottom. With this plan of action, our optimism revives, and we're almost giddy walking this scenic trail. It follows the winding river through the most spectacular vistas of the trip, along the Labyrinth of the Green. Verdant undergrowth and huge cottonwoods, tamarisk, and river willows line the riverbank, their spring green contrasting with towering red sandstone cliffs on both sides. The trail is flat, hot sand, fairly gentle on our sandal-clad feet—until our blisters appear.

Other than occasional birdsong, the morning is very quiet and hot, with no wind. We will have to average three to four miles an hour to reach Spring Canyon before the family leaves their camp. I try to stay in the moment and appreciate this feast for the senses. Suddenly, Deborah stops, looking down at clear animal tracks larger than my hand. "Puma," she whispers. We warily look all around, then hurry on, even more quickly.

We talk of our life views and beliefs, caught as we are in this precarious spot. Deb asks, "What would your teacher say about it?" I leaf through the Buddhist teachings in my memory store.

"Pema would say, 'This situation is workable.'" Picturing my teacher's kind face, I try to "relax as it is," another of her teachings. Remembering Pema's phrase, "come back to the present moment," again and again, as in meditation, I feel less anxious.

Deborah has spent years studying the wisdom of the Taoists, committing many passages from the *Tao Te Ching* to memory. She begins to quote verse after verse, comforting us both with its reassuring instruction.

> *We must visit the dark regions of our mind*
> *the places where our unnamed fears reside.*
> *There we must wait until these fears dissolve.*
> *Then we will return with a light*
> *that will illumine the rest of our path.*

Hours have passed, and we're near the area we think might be Spring Canyon. We've walked about twelve miles so far. Then, a miracle happens! Coming over a rise, we see two backpackers ahead. We hail them and hurry to catch up. They introduce themselves as Maggie and Ed, a newly married couple from Grand Junction, Colorado. They've just ended their weekend camping trip and are headed back to their car, parked at the top of the precipice overlooking Spring Canyon. They listen intently as we explain our plight. Friendly, helpful, and sympathetic, they offer to drive us all the way back to Mineral Bottom to get our car.

There's only one more obstacle for Deb and me. That last mile-and-a-half climb to the crest of the canyon is sheer torture. The trail goes up eight-hundred feet on a steep, narrow, zig-zag track. By now, I have blisters all over my feet. I'm weak from hunger and thirst, exhausted from lack of sleep and the stress of the past twenty-four hours.

It helps that Maggie and Ed are nonstop talkers, regaling us with details of all their outdoor adventures. I can listen quietly, without responding very often. We learn that she's a nurse and he's a lawyer. As they talk and talk, I can privately tune out, silently celebrating our rescue and the magnificent beauty below. This is surely the most striking canyon I've seen so far. Finally dragging ourselves to the canyon rim, we stop to survey an awe-inspiring vista. I breathe thanksgiving for our safe arrival at the top.

An hour later, Ed and Maggie deliver us to Mineral Bottom, luckily right behind a ranger creeping down that incredibly steep road. He takes a thorough report of our canoe and equipment loss and promises to do everything possible to recover it.

By the time Deborah drives her empty Subaru back to The Mayor's House, where we already have a reservation for the night, it's late afternoon. Our host greets us, looking slightly smug. His first words are, "Where's your canoe?"

How did he know? He explains that the rangers just called to say that they have our canoe and all its contents. They guessed where we might be when they found a receipt from the bed-and-breakfast in my billfold. Deborah's unmanned craft was captured downriver by a women's meditation group from Maine. They used it to carry some of their own gear and towed it in. Before we leave Moab, we can pick up all the items that we feared lost, and the Maine group's outfitter will safely store Deb's canoe until she returns here in just two weeks to lead another Naropa wilderness trip.

It couldn't have worked out any better. We lost little—except our overconfidence and pride. We both made serious mistakes and took foolhardy risks. We forgot our tent before a cold, rainy weekend. By traveling too early in May, we had to battle miserable weather and a surging river. Deb perilously jumped into the swirling current to catch an empty canoe, and I had a panic attack. As in classic Greek tragedy, it was hubris for two women, alone, to challenge this river. The Green handed back our nemesis.

Safe in Moab, grateful for *everything*, we take long, hot showers and sleep for the next twelve hours, as tired and dreamless as children after a long day of play. Next morning, we welcome a huge breakfast of French toast and oranges and hot coffee. Even The Mayor seems jolly. It's time to make our way home.

Back in Boulder, Deb phones me early Wednesday with more good news. A couple in Vail found our abandoned gear and her note at Hey Joe. They were four-wheeling on the old mining road on Monday when they noticed our deserted campsite. They rescued everything and called to let Deborah know. She can easily stop by Vail on her next trip to Moab. It's a perfect full circle. We've learned hard, valuable lessons from this most memorable of canoe adventures.

River Karma

$\mathcal{M}$ORE THAN TWENTY YEARS HAVE NOW PASSED SINCE my whitewater initiation in the "Journey to the Source." Countless trips in Colorado, Utah, and Wyoming improved my skills and wilderness education. My mentor, Deborah, led some of these adventures, and I organized others, exploring six navigable rivers—the Colorado, Gunnison, White, Yampa, Green, and North Platte.

Over the years, I developed intimate connection with each river. We hiked to ancient petroglyphs in Ruby and Horse Thief Canyons on the Colorado and enjoyed shady coolness of cottonwood groves on the wild, secluded White. We marveled at the Green River's Labyrinth Canyon and Bowknot Bend. Dominguez Canyon on the Gunnison was a favorite stop, with its waterfall and refreshing swimming holes, carved by water in solid rock.

Towering canyon walls also presided over challenging rapids. A particular one is legendary. Strong current on a sharp dropping curve on the Gunnison is called "Satan's Suckhole." Treacherous rapids heave a canoe toward a deep hole that can pull it into a swirling underwater trap. It is a formidable task to avoid that danger. Through sheer luck, I never tipped completely over, though once my canoe partner and I did slide down backward on that treacherous stretch. I couldn't believe we didn't capsize. Our friends applauded and gave us "style points" for staying afloat.

One sweet memory from many group trips is singing together as we paddled in calm water. Sometimes we barged our canoes together, floating them effortlessly in slow current, literally "going with the flow," as in this song:

> *The river is flowing, flowing and growing.*
> *The river is flowing, down to the sea.*
> *Oh, Mother, carry me, your child I will always be.*
> *Oh, Mother, carry me, down to the sea.*

We sang it like a hymn, feeling our connection with each other and with the river and the soaring cliffs and the whole of nature.

Looking back, the Gunnison River was my favorite. Besides its exciting rapids, extra days in Dominguez Canyon allowed opportunities to spend time alone with the river to reflect on personal meanings. I felt complete interconnection with nature. One early September, the cottonwoods there were just beginning to turn to gold. I memorized the still-life panorama of river and trees from a boulder above the canyon floor where I sat to meditate. That view inspired a poem.

Quiet Time

Sitting like the Buddha
in Dominguez Canyon
I practice my heart's name,

grounded in rock and sky.
Profound silence is broken only
by river rush and canyon wren.
One-seed juniper lays shaded greens
on a dozen desert reds.
A distant totem guards this quiet,
enclosed by ancient sandstone walls.
By the stream below, miniature cottonwoods
try on autumn yellow
lighting the cloudy day like spots of sun.
Desert grasses dry to shades of gray,
the rusty earth textured by last night's rain.
All light is muted now
as earth holds her breath
waiting for winter.
The rock that bears my weight
hosts colonies of microscopic life,
creatures connected,
as I am, to the whole—
all precious, all one.
In deep respect,
I send lotus love to our home
and all who share it—
this heaven, this earth,
this achingly beautiful life.

Besides a fundamental connection with the natural world, canoe trips provided other important life lessons. In canoeing, a basic instruction is to *work with the river,* never against it. Paddling upstream is obviously difficult, indeed impossible for any length of time. Transferred to everyday life, this means that the harder I fight, the more depleted I become. Pushing mercilessly in wrong directions exhausts body, mind, and spirit. Wayne Dyer said it well in *Real Magic*: "Whatever we're *for* strengthens us; whatever we're *against* weakens us."

Canoeing involves keen observation of obstacles, such as rocks and rapids and bends in the channel. Navigating around these hazards requires effective, subtle control with the blade of the paddle. Alertness facilitates safe passage through potentially dangerous situations. In a moment of inattention, a canoe can turn sideways and tip over, so mindfulness is a key protection, just as it is in daily experience. Safe passage requires positive directions, guiding the craft purposely toward the flow of the current, letting the power of the river propel it. Staying present in each moment, we avoid dangerous hazards and glide safely into calmer waters. These are also lessons for managing a satisfying life.

A central teaching is karma, the law of cause and effect. For every action, every thought, there is an effect, a consequence. Clearly, generosity and compassion enhance any successful trip. I remember one good example of the river's "instant karma" that punished an act of arrogance. Our women's group encountered a party of young men canoeing the North Platte in Wyoming. The boys thought it amusing that all these older ladies had the nerve to tackle such a macho sport, especially in the uncertain weather of early spring. With lunch stops and excursions, our two groups passed each other several times during the first day. Ethyl, our favorite guide, knew their leader, and they traded jokes and jesting insults as both parties traveled downriver.

On our second day out, the men passed us very fast, paddling furiously to get in front. It felt like a serious race. Ethyl guessed that they were rushing to beat us to the most desirable camping spot on the river, which she had hoped to claim for our group that night. Sure enough, when we arrived at this welcoming spot, the men were already setting up their camp, terribly smug about their victory in the race. We had to paddle two more tiring hours to put into a decent site on a hill overlooking the channel. That effort took extra discipline and fortitude, hindered by strong headwinds and weariness as we dragged gear uphill. We set up our tents in driving winds that nearly flattened grown women.

But the river spared us after all. A heavy storm hit overnight, bringing more high winds and torrents of cold rain. At 6:00 the next morning, a bedraggled, motley troupe of chastened river rats rounded the bend just as we were crawling out of our dry sleeping bags. We waved in silence as they slid past, already punished by two hours of pre-dawn paddling. Their guide called out that the river had surged during the night and flooded their "perfect" campsite. They had to break camp in pouring rain and hastily retreat to their canoes before daylight. This was river karma. The self-centered behavior of the young men on the North Platte was just one reminder to act with generosity. On many trips, cherished teachings hid behind such mishaps.

I learned to canoe at age fifty. It was perfect timing, just before Jim came out and our lives were forever altered.

Whitewater canoeing transformed me in significant ways, cultivating independence, confidence, courage, outdoor skills, and a keen sense of adventure. I relished reasonable risk and matured as a result. As time passed and my straight spouse crisis faded, I was increasingly certain that I am not alone, not separate from the suffering and joy of others. The river itself became a metaphor for life. Optimistically paddling ahead, not looking back, I could let the river carry me, burdens and all, to the next safe campsite.

Sunset Tapestry

The day seemed slow
till these last rich hours,
more precious as they pass.
Breathing freely now
fresh patterns unfold
in canyon tapestries of light.
A fleeting fabric of solitude
etches soft designs,
blesses this sandstone loom.

Here on this river
I know.
My time has rushed,
tumbled in incessant waves
breaking on eroding shores.
Constant rapids
chattered over rocks
drowned in swirling holes.

Paddling westward now
ripples unfold
in calmer waters.
The setting sun weaves
tranquil visions
on the western horizon,
flashing orange to softer gold
to quiet gray—
fabric of solitude,
colors of calm
wrapping me close
in night's soft embrace.
Canyon walls endure
water, wind, fire, and time.
They stand still,
teach peace.

Pebbles in the Stream

Childhood family fun at Grand Lake was the ground for my adult fascination with large bodies of water. My enthusiasm for canoeing is perhaps the clearest example, although halcyon days waterskiing at Lake Powell, exotic travels seeking intimate connection with dolphins and stingrays, and my peaceful practice of Watsu are similar instances. In each of these pursuits, and during multiple cruises and sailing trips to the Caribbean, Hawaiian, and Tahitian Islands, I felt joyous in and on water.

I began to recognize that my passion for these pursuits represents an innate longing to merge with the mysterious Whole, represented in part by water. At times when I felt lost and alone, those trips were reassuring. A nebulous desire to be at one with the greater universe reinforced my ties to ocean, lake, river, and pool. The sale of the *Temptation,* our Lake Powell houseboat, was a painful loss. I was also sad to give up my warm Watsu pool and abandon that compassionate therapeutic practice. Age and injuries interfered after a dozen years of canoeing, and I missed the thrill of those journeys as well. Reluctantly loosening my grasp on these treasured pursuits, I began to understand that my pain was not entirely from the loss of the object or experience itself but from *clinging* to that which is, by its nature, only temporary. Like my former, predictable life, none of these pastimes could last. Just as the Buddha taught, I had to let go to be free.

Starting over at mid-life involved risky experiments. I was engaged in a compulsory process of personal reinvention. Memorable adventures created sporadic flashes, like a stream that carries bright pebbles with an undercurrent of spiritual inquiry in the continuous flow of time.

Writing to Heal

THE PUBLICATION OF *My Husband Is Gay* DRAMATICALLY altered the rest of my life. Its reception revealed a definitive calling—to use what I learned from harsh experience to extend healing and hope to other straight spouses. When Jim disclosed his homosexuality, I desperately needed a book of informed encouragement. No such book existed at that time, so I determined to write it myself.

My first draft was a rant, a torrent of pent-up frustration, anger, and retribution. It was terrible! I had to get that unprintable poison out of my system first. I put that manuscript on a closet shelf for a whole year, while I proceeded with the more urgent need to restore my emotional balance and self-esteem. I threw myself into therapy, joined a straight spouse support group, confided in close friends, studied the dharma, and engaged in challenging outdoor adventures. This was essential grounding for an emerging vocation.

When I regained clearer perspective, it was time to write again. This time, I would focus on other straight spouses' experiences, not just my own. I networked and even advertised for subjects to interview, finding thirty-five women willing to reveal their intimate stories. I rewrote my manuscript three more times, gleaning wisdom from my subjects' diverse histories. Each successive version came closer to my vision of a tool for recovery. The result was the nonfiction book, *My Husband Is Gay: A Woman's Guide to Surviving the Crisis.*

When the manuscript seemed presentable, I followed all the rules of the day, meticulously preparing sparkling query letters and a flawless book proposal to entice a literary agent to represent me. Two disheartening rejections from agents jolted me into reality. Clearly, there was little demand for an unknown, previously unpublished author, writing on a controversial subject.

Undaunted, I determined to skip the search for an agent and approach small publishers directly. Almost by accident, I came across an outdated catalog from a small California publisher, The Crossing Press. Their catalog offered an eclectic mix of titles, many related to alternative lifestyles and healing, but they listed nothing specific for straight spouses. I was still stinging from my previous rejections, but decided to gamble once again. With little expectation of success, I sent the publisher a query letter. Just a week later, I got a response. I had an actual phone call from the President of The Crossing Press!

"I received your letter describing your book on straight spouse recovery. I'm interested in that topic, and I'd like to see your manuscript."

I almost fainted. To hear directly from the publisher herself, only a few days after my initial query, and to have a request for the whole manuscript—impossible! Unheard of to skip the usual interim steps of a meticulous book proposal. When I recovered my voice, I thanked her for her quick reply and promised to send the manuscript immediately.

Two weeks passed. Then she called again. "We want to publish your book."

Her matter-of-fact acceptance and the speed of the transaction defied any rational expectation. However, as our conversation unfolded, I learned the reason for her deep interest. She herself was a straight spouse, having remained with her gay husband after his disclosure. She nursed him through his final years until his eventual death. Like me, she had an abiding interest in helping other wounded women find a positive path to recovery.

She offered a $5,000 advance against royalties and promised to engage an author's publicist to attract media attention. Her abrupt acceptance of a manuscript from a novice was incredibly rare. Out of thousands of small presses, it was a miraculous coincidence for me to connect with this perfect match. Naïvely, I didn't realize that such support was utterly exceptional, even in 2001. I had no means to measure her generosity at the time. Fortunately, the publisher recognized a ready market for a book on this niche topic, and her instinct was sound.

The Boston publicist she hired was also amazingly effective. She opened opportunities for more than seventy live radio interviews in the United States and England and television appearances on network news and talk shows. During the next two years, I traveled to Chicago and New York to appear on *The Oprah Winfrey Show*, *Good Morning America*, *The Early Show*, *Inside Edition*, and the *Today Show*. I had live interviews with Diane Sawyer, Iyanla, and Anderson Cooper. For years after that, each time some married celebrity came out, shocking a straight mate, I was called by the media to comment or interview.

Our initial publicity campaign escalated into a demanding round of appearances for this formerly camera-shy introvert. At every opportunity, I carried the message that there is no shame in being a straight spouse. We are legion. "You are not alone" was the mantra that helped me and thousands of others to heal. "You can move beyond your disappointment to reshape a thriving future." I also conveyed a conviction that grew from my own experience: forgiveness is the final remedy to heal one's own wounds. That, with the "tincture of time," opens opportunity for a better future. These internalized perceptions restored my own health and well-being as well.

My Husband Is Gay was published in the U.S. in 2001. A year later, when my book was becoming old news in the United States and I had begun to relax, I had an unforeseen phone call from a woman with a foreign accent. She identified herself as "Boom, calling from Bangkok." She was a Thai journalist with the Bangkok daily English-language newspaper, *The Nation,* engaged by an independent publisher to translate my book. Boom was putting final touches on her Thai translation, but she was puzzled about some Americanisms in the original. "What is *Leave It to Beaver*?" she wondered. (I had referenced that title of a 1950s television series to describe my early married years with Jim: purely conventional, mid-American family life.) Chuckling about Boom's confusion over this strange American phrase, I hung up the phone and wondered where this would lead. I had no idea what fantastic experiences lay ahead.

That short conversation was my first notice that my American publisher had sold foreign rights for my book. The Thai translation would be published by Cyberfish Media, a tiny company jointly owned by three journalists—two Thai, one American. A second surprising call came a few weeks later from Paul Bradley, the American partner with Cyberfish. He asked me to write a personal message for Thai readers, an author's preface with a warm greeting and statement of purpose. That was exciting enough, but his next request was stunning. He invited me to fly to Bangkok in October to help launch their translated version. In contrast to my previous American publicity efforts, which were spread over two years, this would be a full-scale, intense, condensed campaign in less than a month, climaxing at the Thai national book expo. Could I come to Thailand? Of course!

I had only a few days to write the introduction that Paul requested. How would Thai women differ from the people I had interviewed? What similarities could be assumed? My objective was to create connection, to tap universal needs and desires that cross boundaries of culture and language. The tone should be welcoming, as if reaching for the hand of a friend. For the first time, I realized that this first book was establishing my true vocation of writing to heal.

A Personal Message for Thai Readers from Carol Grever

Sawaddee. What a privilege it is to welcome readers in Thailand to the pages of my book. Though I am an American and wrote originally for readers in English-speaking countries, I believe that the core experiences of the people in this book will be familiar to you too. One out of five gay men is or has been married to a straight wife. And one out of ten husbands is bisexually active. Clearly, homosexuality is a fact of life worldwide; one's innate sexual identity is not dependent on country of origin. The ideas in this book may therefore be as helpful to a woman in Bangkok as they are to a woman in Chicago or London.

There has already been some indication that the book's message reaches over geographic boundaries. I have been amazed by the warm reception readers gave the original version. Interviewing more than seventy-five times with networked radio and television programs in the U.S. and England, I encountered great curiosity about this phenomenon of a heterosexual women being married for many years (unknowingly) to a homosexual man. I was highly motivated in those interviews to reach a wider audience with my thesis that the discovery that one's husband is gay doesn't necessarily destroy the possibility of future happiness for either partner. I wanted to offer practical information, common experience, recognition, empathy, and hope.

Letters I've received from women in the United States, Canada, England, and Australia echo familiar themes. They demonstrate that people have more similarities than differences in matters of the heart and issues of family. We all share a need to love and be loved, to feel secure in the companionship of marriage, to protect our children, and to trust our partner. When that trust is betrayed, we feel deep pain, loss, fear, anger, and despair. Thai wives may have different outer circumstances, but like their English-speaking sisters, their hearts can be broken—and eventually healed.

The purpose of my book is to lead to that healing. An alert reader can translate its content into a Thai environment. Relieving isolation is imperative. Support groups and the Internet are valuable resources. I also have a website at www.carolgrever.com that links to additional sites.

It is an honor to welcome Thai readers to my little book. I offer it with greatest respect, affirming warm feelings about your country's ancient connection with Buddhism. Reared in a Christian home, I came to the Buddhist path during my years of adjustment after my husband came out, so my spiritual way is strongly tied to that turning point. Sitting meditation grounded me as I rested in Basic Goodness and calmed the chatter in my mind. The myth of separation is dispelled; I know that all is one and I can accept what is. Through practice, I stepped out of the past and into the present moment. The result is my path; Buddhist practice has given me the courage to walk that path with joy and patience. As many women in my book demonstrate, spiritual grounding is the single most important resource for renewal after any crisis. For me, Buddhism's gentle wisdom offers the tools to use my experience as fuel for waking up. It has enriched my life immeasurably and I'm grateful.

It is with this gratitude that I share the experiences of 26 American women, with a fervent desire to help straight spouses in your country too. I hope someday to visit your beautiful homeland and walk this path with you, both physically and spiritually. We are not so different after all, so I invite you to turn the page, to learn from other women, and to know that you are not alone.

—CAROL GREVER

2002

I did travel to Thailand for the book launch, an exciting, exhausting, *unique* experience. After that trip, I was inspired to broaden my work with straight spouse recovery and engage in peer counseling with other mixed-orientation couples. My psychologist friend, Dr. Deborah Bowman, and I later coauthored *When Your Spouse Comes Out: A Straight Mate's Recovery*

Manual. It was published as a textbook in 2008 by Taylor & Francis. That same year, I wrote and produced a related documentary, *One Gay, One Straight: Complicated Marriages.* My blog, *Straight Spouse Connection,* carries articles, book reviews, and guest comments on related subjects. This purpose-driven work has opened many opportunities over two decades to advocate for straight spouses through media, public speaking, and contributions to academic texts and periodicals. Devotion to a higher calling of helping others cope with the challenges of mixed-orientation relationships transformed my own life. Writing to heal became my vocation.

Taste of Fame

October 4, Friday

THE FIVE-STAR SHANGRI-LA HOTEL IS SPECTACULAR— one of the most luxurious in Thailand. From our room on the fourteenth floor, we look down on the Chao Phraya River's busy, complex activity, like a freeway on water. It's quiet up here, a welcome respite after two full days of flying from Denver to L.A., to Tokyo, to Bangkok. I'm deeply grateful to be here, and even more thankful that I'm not traveling alone. My good friend, Linda, jumped at the chance to come along to help with logistics. I wouldn't have tackled this challenge without a reliable companion.

We're here in Bangkok to introduce the Thai translation of my book, *My Husband Is Gay.* We only had a few hours of sleep after our two-day journey, but a sumptuous buffet breakfast at the hotel restored us enough to explore a bit. We boarded the boat shuttle to River Center, a high-rise shopping center. After exploring a few shops, we rode the boat back to the hotel, enjoyed a drink at their riverside bar, and returned to the room to rest. Tonight, at last, we'll meet with the architects of this publicity tour, the three partners of Cyberfish Media. We'll have dinner together at A Matter of Taste restaurant, where my first book event will be held on Wednesday.

Paul is the managing director of Cyberfish. He's a New York journalist who has worked all over Asia. He met his gay partner, Yord, when they both wrote for *The Nation*, the Bangkok English-language daily. The two of them discovered my book while browsing a gay bookstore in Philadelphia and decided to publish a translation. Such converging coincidences continue to amaze me. Paul is tall and boyish-looking, with the worst haircut I've ever seen. He is perpetually rumpled looking, but he's so personable that I immediately like him a lot.

Yord is also tall, a native of Bangkok, and quite handsome. Their third partner in Cyberfish Media is Boom, whose original phone call alerted me to this opportunity. Boom is a dynamo, originally from the southern peninsula of Thailand. We learn that English nicknames, like Boom, are typical in Thailand. Vivacious and attractive, she is married to the Australian ambassador here. The three publishing partners became friends as colleagues at *The Nation*. Now, Boom serves as marketing director for Cyberfish, while finishing a master's degree in international relations.

I'm thrilled to hold an actual copy of the Thai version of my book. It has a feminine, embossed cover design in lavender and pink on white. The Thai print inside resembles delicate calligraphy, giving the pages a soft appearance different from books in English. Leafing through it for the first time, I realize that this book is more than my private concept—it's now a reality. It is already being sold all over Bangkok, even in a multitude of kiosks at Skytrain stations. I sign fifty copies for Yord to take to the first gay-lesbian film festival here. That event will be held at the German Cultural Center, starting on Saturday.

Our dinner with the team is fun, with no awkwardness at all. I have some difficulty understanding Yord and Boom, with their heavy Thai accents. But we soon chat like old friends. Linda and I also enjoy our first taste of the decidedly peppery Thai food. It is much hotter and spicier than American versions. Despite our travel fatigue, it's a great evening. Now, we'll have the weekend free to rest and explore Bangkok. Linda has already booked a half-day tour to the Grand Palace and the Temple of the Emerald Buddha.

October 5, Saturday

Our tour guide, Pom, is a sweet, sincere Buddhist who delights in escorting visitors around this centerpiece of Bangkok, the palace of the Rama kings. It is unbelievably ornate—like nothing I've seen anywhere else. There are many complex buildings vying for attention, each more elaborately decorated than the last. It is a sensory feast of gilt and shiny tile and brilliant colors and inlaid mirrors and porcelain flowers. Our photos capture only tiny impressions. The whole is much greater than the parts.

Like the Grand Palace, the interior of the Temple of the Emerald Buddha defies description. It has a layered gold shrine soaring fifty feet high. At each level, there are multiple buddhas and bodhisattvas and elaborate carvings and prayer wheels. Perched on the top is a golden shrine in which the Emerald Buddha sits. The famous statue is deep green with gold accents. Its name comes from its emerald color, but the statue is actually carved from a single piece of jade. The huge shrine is crowded with multiple paintings and statues. It would take hours to examine each one closely. Together, the collection commands overwhelming awe.

People here seem very sincere about their religion, deeply immersed in Theravadan Buddhism. Their ascetic path informs their national character. There are thirty thousand temples in the country. Every neighborhood in Bangkok has one. From any high place, the temples' bright tile roofs with "sky hooks" on top stand out, scattered among office buildings and ordinary houses.

After meditating in the shrine room of the Emerald Buddha, Linda and I visit the Temple of the Golden Buddha. It is a large statue made of pure gold, valued at U.S. $14 million. When the Burmese were warring with Thailand, stealing valuables and destroying many temples, the monks covered this statue with stucco to hide its value. They did such a good cover-up that it took two hundred years to rediscover this treasure. When the people moved the statue to a new temple, some of the stucco cracked, revealing shining gold beneath.

We have used our rare day off very well, seeing some of the most famous sites in Bangkok. Refreshed by a swim and a quick nap, we have dinner reservations at the hotel's traditional Thai restaurant, housed in three teak buildings on the riverfront. In each of the dining areas, patrons are entertained by elegant dancers in elaborate traditional costumes. The Thai people are delicately beautiful, lithe and graceful. Their famous "Thai smile" lights the room.

Sunday is rainy, but we want to see as much of Bangkok as possible before I "go to work" with Cyberfish. Today, we'll visit Ayutthaya Province, north of Bangkok. Our first stop is at Bang Pa-In Palace, a fantastically elaborate Chinese palace, dating back to the seventeenth century. A dozen elegant buildings are completely furnished and kept in perfect, original condition. Walking the grounds, we admire manicured gardens and water features. The complex is reminiscent of Versailles and other royal grounds in Europe.

Riding a bus through the province, we encounter heavy flooding that has ruined thousands of homes along the Chao Phraya River. People are camping on higher ground, while the water stands in their houses. It is a pitiful sight. Even the highway is covered with water as we drive through low spots. Several major temples in the area are inaccessible because they are also flooded.

At last, we arrive at the ancient capital of Ayutthaya. It was the center of the country's government until it was destroyed by the Burmese. The ruins have been preserved and serve as a national monument. Its spiritual atmosphere remains, its long history worn like a cloak over crumbling ruins of temples and stupas. Monks and nuns maintain these grounds, and the newer temple is still in use. I drop out of the tour group for a meditative walk alone, circling through the broken pieces of the venerable site.

Our bus takes an expressway back to the river for a boat ride back to Bangkok. On board the *Horizon,* we find a four-course lunch, with traditional Thai foods and Singha beer, the local favorite. It is light, with a slight floral hint and no bitter aftertaste. (Another beer called Chang is forty percent alcohol! I won't try that one.) Seeing Bangkok and its surroundings from the vantage point of the river is distinctly different from the city's noisy streets. Now, my thoughts turn to tomorrow. I'll need to be ready for my first Thai television appearance early in the morning. I'm excited and a bit nervous.

October 7, Monday

Early morning! It's pouring rain when Boom picks us up at 6:00 to drive to the studio for my live television interview. Streets are flooded, and traffic is incredibly snarled. I've never experienced traffic like this. It's hard to see through lashing curtains of rain. Boom drives through the hellish traffic, answering her cell phone while talking to us—never seeming ruffled.

During long traffic stops, I ask about her family. She speaks English with an Australian accent, learned from her Aussie husband. They met in the Solomon Islands, married, have a young daughter, and divide their time between Bangkok and Australia. Her husband is in the diplomatic corps, and the family lives in the government compound. Boom says she and Yord have been "best girlfriends" since working together at *The Nation,* along with Paul.

We arrive at the studio by 7:00 and wait in a dingy locker room till the makeup/hair team calls me in. They quickly have me painted and ready for the cameras. (I must say I am repelled by their use of the same lip brush on everyone. Trapped, with no escape from it!)

Baan Lek Thi Ha interviews, with Boom as my translator. This daily, live show is comparable to our *Today* or *Good Morning, America*. The interview is like a tennis match, as I sit in the middle on a couch, looking from side to side to face first the interviewer, then Boom. The show's set is formal and elegant, like a *House Beautiful* parlor. Baan is a former movie star, still strikingly attractive. Her interview is necessarily superficial, lasting only ten minutes, but I'm relieved to have this first one behind me.

Our next publicity stop is at the Jim Thompson House in Surawong for a noon press interview. We're seated at a table in the teak lounge at the Jim Thompson complex, sipping cold drinks as we speak with the reporter. His interview is much more extensive than the one this morning, and it seems to go well.

While we're here, Linda and I take the opportunity to tour the Jim Thompson home after my interview. It is a remodeled complex of seven old Thai teakwood houses, put together like a jigsaw puzzle. Fabulously wealthy from the silk trade, Thompson mysteriously disappeared while hiking in Cambodia at age sixty-one. He enjoyed his unusual home for only eight years. Still completely intact, the house showcases an extensive collection of art and porcelain and exotic furnishings from all over Asia. It is an uncommon museum.

Walking to the Skytrain to return to the hotel, I have my first taste of celebrity. Two men sit at a sidewalk café as we pass. Suddenly one man jumps up from his chair, points at me, and says, "I saw you on television this morning!" Then he points at Boom. "I saw you, too!" His enthusiasm and excitement are stunning.

October 8, Tuesday

Paul arrives at the Shangri-La at 8:30 to have breakfast with us before the day's events. Boom is also here to help me prepare for the *Before Monday* TV taping, to be aired next Sunday evening on Channel 9.

The film crew has set up in the garden just outside our Krungthep Wing of the hotel. The garden faces the Chao Phraya and has a shrine and palm trees in the background. It's lush and exotic, hot and breezy. River noises are screened out by the microphones. I'm impressed with the professionalism of this interviewer, Anuchit Jureegasa, managing director of VIP: Video International Production Group. Having studied for eight years in Hartford, Connecticut, he speaks impeccable English. He's tall, slim, and handsome. His wife assists him in the productions, and both have read my book. In our conversation before the interview, I learn that Anuchit's sister is a straight spouse, married for twenty years before her husband came out. She never recovered from the shock and has been ill since. This explains the family's keen interest in my work.

Anuchit's questions are sensitive and intelligent. My Buddhist conversion is of particular interest, though my Tibetan Mahayana practice differs from their Theravadan tradition. People here are curious about an American Buddhist of any stripe, and I thoroughly enjoy our conversation.

I notice that Paul has been preoccupied all morning, saying little at breakfast. After the video crew leaves, he drops his bomb. Last Friday, the day Linda and I arrived, he had a routine physical to renew his visa. His doctors diagnosed a malignant tumor. Paul will have his whole right kidney removed this Thursday morning! His friend, Jane Vejjajiva, the publisher's agent Cyberfish engaged, helped him make speedy arrangements with the influence of her parents, both respected Bangkok MDs. Paul is understandably apprehensive but maintains a brave and cheerful front.

Our afternoon is free, so Linda and I try to absorb Paul's upsetting news during a visit to Wat Pho, the temple of the famous Reclining Buddha. (*Wat* means temple in Thai.) The huge Buddha is gold-leafed and magnificent, the soles of the feet inlaid with intricate mother of pearl designs. Extensive temple grounds surround several museums and salas, open air porticos with statues of buddhas.

Wat Pho is also the home of the Traditional Thai Massage School. Thai massage is famous for its herbal wash, assisted stretches, and deep tissue work, similar to shiatsu. Tired from a long day, we decide to try it. We change into loose, short pajamas. Bags of hot, yellow herbs are scrubbed all over our bodies, turning our skin golden. Therapists use pressure points and lean their own weight against us to deepen rejuvenating stretches. I love the lingering calm relaxation that lasts all evening.

October 9, Wednesday

Mealtime in Thailand is an adventure in itself. Each day at the hotel, Linda and I enjoy the breakfast buffet, usually making it the first of two meals for the day. The buffet boasts wondrous exotic fruits, the most unusual called "dragon fruit." It has incredibly bright pink skin, thick and scaly (like a dragon), with pure white, soft inside pulp dotted with tiny black seeds. The fruit's mild taste isn't remarkable, but its appearance startles. I prefer the rose apples and Asian pears, both very crisp and tart.

Dining seems less formal here than in many western homes. White Japanese rice is placed in the center of the plate, and several different savory foods are served around the edges. The utensils are also used differently. The fork is held in the left hand to push food into a large oval spoon, held in the right. Several foods are put together for a bite, taken from the spoon. Thais enjoy a combination of distinct tastes taken together. The spoon is also used to cut food, rather than a knife. It's actually very efficient. Foods are spicy, often with lots of garlic, basil, and hot peppers. Soups are common, often with a noodle base. All courses—salad, soup and entrée—are put on the table together. Even a daily meal is an exotic experience here!

Today, we'll meet Jane Vejjajiva, the publisher's agent, at a venerable Thai restaurant, the Baan Khanitha on Soi Ruamrudee. Jane is a tiny woman, confined to a wheelchair, disabled since birth by a wasting muscular disorder. Despite her handicap, she is highly educated and has earned prestigious scholarships and academic recognition. Today, Jane is our charming hostess at a two-hour lunch. She delights in showing us how to enjoy a half-dozen exotic Thai foods that she selects for us. It's all delicious, and we appreciate further education in Thai cuisine and customs. Since Linda and I both like to cook (and eat), it's fun to try these new foods.

After our elaborate lunch with Jane, we drive to A Matter of Taste, the venue for our official book launch event. This is my first meeting with the Bangkok press, a focus of the Cyberfish team's effort for weeks leading up to my visit. I had prayed that a few press people might attend. Imagine my elation when fifty reporters come and I'm facing at least twenty cameras all at once. I feel like a rock star!

For the presentation, four of us stand up front, with reporters filling the rest of the room. Boom and I are joined by a psychiatrist who works with sexual issues and a moderator, Sarawanee, a savvy friend of Boom's. Sarawanee studied art education in Chicago and has flawless English. A huge replica of my book's cover forms a backdrop on the wall behind us. The reporters' questions are relatively superficial, but afterward I am able to elaborate during a private interview with Tanita Saenkhum from *The Nation*. Pauline, a beautiful Chinese public relations expert and a friend of Boom's, is there to help clarify our conversation. This interview is deep and sensitive. A week from now it will become a half-page feature with a color picture, published on the back cover of section one of this important daily newspaper.

The launch event feels triumphant! Our Cyberfish team drives to Boom's home to relax and meet her husband, James. They live in a rather stark apartment, surprising in its austerity. Their daughter, five-year-old Jamie, greets us. After a drink and a quiet chat, we go to dinner at the Yok Yor, a seafood restaurant across the river from the Shangri-La. It's a casual, open-air affair on the river, perfect after our vigorous day. I want to treat the group tonight but tease the others that they have to sing for their supper. Boom and Yord are karaoke fanatics and eagerly take the challenge, singing along with recorded American hits. I'm amazed at the bill. Dinner with wine for six cost just U.S. $45.

October 10, Thursday

Paul's surgery is scheduled this morning, and we won't be able to see him for a couple of days. Linda and I are on our own. We sleep late and then plan our "day off." We decide to visit the Erawan Shrine, highly revered by generations of Thais. We can catch the Skytrain across the street from our hotel.

Transportation in Bangkok is difficult, unless you use the Skytrain or the river. Both of those means are fast and pleasant.

The Skytrain is like a subway train, only it runs on tracks built high above the streets. Trains come every five minutes and travel very fast. Boats, like river buses, run every ten or fifteen minutes on the Chao Phraya. They stop frequently on public piers. The changing scene is interesting, and the breeze is cool, so this is a pleasant way to move through the city.

Travel on the street is a different matter. There are sixty thousand taxis in the city and almost three million cars. At rush hours, the traffic jams are horrific—one may sit for an hour in a single spot. A red light may last ten minutes or more. Surprisingly, there is almost no horn honking. People are resigned to wait in cars, but motorbikes buzz around at terrifying speeds. Dozens at a time pass by. Tuk-tuks, the golf-cart-like truck-taxis, are scattered in the lanes, with riders choking on blue exhaust.

At all times, the air is laden with fumes. Pollution is so bad it can affect the intelligence of children. Traffic congestion and poor air quality are two of the greatest problems in daily life here. Many people wear masks on the street, especially those who work outside, such as traffic policemen and street cleaners. The air also smells of sewer gas. Pedestrians walk at their own risk, dodging cars, tuk-tuks, motorbikes, and holes in the narrow, uneven sidewalks (where sidewalks exist at all). It's hard to be outdoors here.

Then there is the noise! Vehicle motors, especially from motorbikes, tug boats, diesel-run longboats, river taxies on the Chao Phraya, loud music, people talking on ubiquitous cell phones, and construction work—an unrelenting din. Retreating into a quiet, insulated Skytrain offers brief relief.

Our elevated train ride is fun, as we whiz at great speed. We get off at Siam Station, and soon we are at the Grand Hyatt Erawan Hotel, named for the famous shrine adjacent to it. We learn that a Rotary Club is meeting there at noon and decide to visit their meeting. I have our club banner to exchange with theirs, a custom for visiting Rotarians in other countries.

The presence of women is unusual in the male-dominated chapter. We're treated politely but cause a stir as we take our places at the luncheon table. We are the only females present. Unlike our meetings at home, everything here is formal and highly structured. Each officer has a Rotary business card with his club history (chairmanships, offices) listed. Their three-course lunch has a specially printed menu and is served formally by waiters. The speaker is the founder of a university, obviously a notable dignitary. I am seated next to a former District Governor and introduce myself as a past president of Boulder Rotary. He's amazed to learn that a woman has held that office in a three-hundred-member club. As we continue talking, I begin to relax and feel relatively welcome (even if I am a woman).

After the Rotary meeting, Linda and I explore the Erawan Shrine area. The shrine and grounds are crowded with devotees, shrouded in incense smoke. After watching traditional Thai dancers perform outside, we shop at the mall for gifts to take to our families, and end our day with a cool, fresh salad back at the Shangri-La pool.

October 11, Friday

Opening events for the National Book Fair begin today. The semi-annual event is held at the Queen Sirikit National

Convention Center. I was supposed to attend the opening, but at the last minute our plans changed because of the requirement for security clearance and no time to get it. Security is tight because the Crown Princess will be present to open the fair. The expo will last for ten days. Last March 300,000 visitors attended. Vendors sold two million books at that last fair.

The big news for me today is that my little book is Se-Ed's number two best seller. Paul is elated that Bangkok's premier bookstore is that impressed. Besides their main store in Siam Center, they have kiosks in hundreds of Skytrain stations all over the city. Yord called to say that he took pictures of their display at a Skytrain station as proof. To celebrate, Boom will throw a dinner party at her home. After we arrive, Boom announces that she's arranged a live radio interview for 10:30 that night! It is to last a whole hour. Can I stay awake? For better or worse, at 10:00 we set out, Boom's friend driving like a kamikaze pilot, weaving through frightful traffic. We miss a turn and arrive late at the station, but the interview will air anyway.

Despite my misgivings about this unexpected event, it's great fun. The action is frenetic: Boom is translator, Yord is interviewer, and the show's host is chief *interrupter*. Another of Boom's friends, Pauline, slips in late to join Linda and our driver as our live audience outside the studio's glass window. They cheer us on and gesture through the glass. After much hilarity, probably fueled by the wine we had with dinner, we end the program with listener questions, some of which make no sense at all. But we keep talking! I really wonder how many people actually listen to programs like that.

October 12, Saturday

Linda and I hurry to the hospital to meet Yord and visit Paul. The three of us stand awkwardly around his bed, Paul peering up from the green hospital sheets. He looks surprisingly alert, though we learn that the cancer had gone beyond his kidney. The doctors scheduled CAT scans and bone scans to see if it has metastasized.

Yord's friend, a gay monk, is also supposed to meet us here. Soon he appears, wearing his saffron robes and sandals and carrying a bright pink cloth bag for his papers and books. Having read my book in Thai, Phra Chai Waradhammo traveled more than two hours by bus to see us. His monastery is at Kien Khate Temple, outside Bangkok in Pathumthani Province.

His sincere eagerness to talk with me is touching. He is thirty-four years old, from a very large Thai family. Only two of his sisters, one of whom is lesbian, know of his homosexual orientation. He is isolated from the others by the certainty that they would reject him if they knew. He's an extremely thin, drawn up, sad little man, but passionate about his advocacy of gays and lesbians in a support group and class he teaches. He's also a writer, using a pen name to publish articles on gay-related issues for a newsletter and on-line community. His English is limited, but he tries hard to understand me. His whole skinny forehead wrinkles into a knot over little horn-rimmed glasses. It's his habitual expression, I think, for the lines are already etched on his young face.

Phra Chai is hungry for information and burdened by the prejudice in his own environment. I give him a gift of Celestial Seasonings Tea and a little book about compassion. He responds with a photo of an ancient Buddha face carved into the massive roots of a banyan tree near Ayutthaya. We share family pictures, with Yord translating our conversation. One photo shows the monk with some of his siblings, sitting in front of his monastery. Pointing out the two sisters who know and accept his homosexuality, he speaks of his sadness that he can't tell his parents and wonders especially if Jim's mother still loves him. This sad monk's painful isolation is palpable; I'm moved by his openness with a stranger from a foreign land. We talk for nearly two hours in the coffee shop at the hospital. Phra Chai touches my heart.

October 13, Sunday

Our main activity for today is a visit to the people's weekend market. We ride the Skytrain to its very end and walk into a *huge* flea market that must cover a square mile. It has literally hundreds (maybe thousands) of small shops, huddled under contiguous tin roofs. This market is where locals buy practically everything, from plants to blue jeans to jewelry to silks. It is unbelievably hot and humid under the tin roof.

Soon, Linda and I are melting and miserable. We escape outside and walk toward the Skytrain stop. A few yards from the market entrance, I witness a sight so horrifying that it will be etched forever in my mind. A deformed man writhes on his belly, bobbing his head up and down off the filthy, scorched street in front of the market. His bandaged, terribly twisted limbs splay out in fantastic directions, thin as broomsticks, totally useless. He makes pitiful noises as everyone walks past, seemingly oblivious. I avert my gaze, and feel guilty for doing so.

Beggars are the most dismaying sight on these streets. Like this pitiful man, they are often incredibly deformed. Disabled people who live on the street are common here. Locals totally ignore them, sometimes stepping over them without a pause. How they survive at all is a mystery. Is there so little public sympathy because of a cultural belief that these unfortunates are living out bad karma, that they deserve to suffer to expiate previous crimes? Is there reluctance to interfere with a person's retribution for past lives' transgressions? Similarly, gays are thought to be made that way as punishment for womanizing in past lives. That is their payback, their karma. In Thailand, this might explain the public's disparagement of homosexuals, even though there is general acceptance of other diversity. To a western mind, used to social systems that try to assist people in need, these attitudes are confusing and disturbing.

A similar phenomenon on Bangkok streets is the presence everywhere of "soi dogs," or street strays. (Soi means road). They are fed garbage in alleys by some restaurants, so don't appear to be starving, but they are exceedingly mangy and pathetic. No one cares for them and they lie around and scratch themselves bloody. There are a few stray cats, but not many—also unkempt, but generally in better shape than the poor dogs.

So we hurry back "home" to the clean and safe Shangri-La. We end our day watching the "Before Monday" TV interview, taped the previous Tuesday at the hotel. It was our best publicity effort here, without need of an interpreter. Linda is also interviewed briefly on that show, giving a friend's perspective. She is great—so direct and honest. She is natural and believable. The program also interweaves segments from the book launch interview, which creates a complete message. I am greatly relieved that this most important program looks good.

October 14, Monday

Boom joins us for breakfast at the Shangri-La before we leave for the book expo at 9:00. I'm scheduled for a panel onstage with a host and the Thai translator of the *Ya Ya Sisterhood*, a popular American novel about southern women's middle-age crises. I don't understand the connection between the two books, but go along with the program. The host is utterly ill-prepared and immature; he seems like a puerile disc jockey. My translator is clearly embarrassed by the host's superficial, repetitious questions.

It's disappointing that my initial expo opportunity feels wasted. However, one woman sitting in the audience connects with me through broad smiles and nods as I speak. I believe she must be a straight spouse. That singular connection helps balance the substandard interview. When it finally ends, I hurry down to approach her. As we touch hands, she confirms my impression. She expresses gratitude for my book and whispers heartfelt "thanks."

Following my interview, I busily sign books at the large Se-Ed Bookstore booth. During that first hour, we sell about 30 books and I speak with three women in some depth. Their eyes reveal their wounds. They know what I write about. My inscription on each book reads, "The result is the path." I hope they understand.

After working the expo, Linda and I have only an hour at the hotel to dress for our evening treat—a dinner cruise on the Chao Phraya, alone with Boom and James. The river at night is magical: all lights against blackness. At night you can't see the air pollution, and the moist breeze is cool and refreshing.

James is a thoroughly kind, gentle man who loves his wife with obvious passion. He gazes at Boom with touching sweetness. He's the self-made son of a poor coal-miner, from a family of six boys. He vowed to escape the dark bowels of the mine through education, becoming a scholar, former teacher, enthusiastic pilot, Vietnam vet, and now a diplomat. He's also a devoted father to little Jamie, and a supportive, admiring husband to Boom. It was good to know him better. After spending our full day with Boom, Linda and I at last bid them goodnight and gather our thoughts for the next magazine interview tomorrow.

October 15, Tuesday

Two major interviews are scheduled for our last full day before Linda and I take a short recovery break. I can't express how essential Linda's presence is, here in Bangkok. She has been my constant companion through good and bad, hard and sweet experiences, from the grueling flights to get here, through two weeks of hard, exhilarating work. She's carried my purse and camera, encouraged me when I was tired or nervous, observed details I missed, acted as our travel planner, consulted, advised, and enjoyed it all. She's a great travel buddy and a generous friend. Without Linda, I wouldn't have been brave enough to come to Thailand at all. I would have missed this greatest opportunity of my professional life.

At 9:00 a.m., Boom meets us downstairs in the Shangri-La front lounge. It's a lavish public area with massive chairs, two-story windows facing the river, and beautiful Asian art on either end. Bigger than life engravings are amazingly detailed, etched in gold on a black background, framed in carved cinnabar. I feel dwarfed by this elegant setting.

Boom again translates for the interviewer, who probably understands more English than she lets on. Her magazine, *Kwan Ruen,* is an important one, in circulation since the 1970's. It was a pioneering publication, equivalent to our *New Yorker.* She offers me a sample copy. It's an inch thick and full of major advertisers. My article will be in their "newsmaker" feature interview, a coup for an obscure author like me.

By late morning, we finish our work for *Kwan Ruen.* Boom prepares us for one more appearance, a television interview this evening with two psychiatrists who specialize in sex issues. I have already met both doctors and the show's host at the book launch event. The interview and discussion go smoothly, again with our lively Boom translating. It's an opportunity to share information about the Straight Spouse Network, and I encourage them to start a similar support group here in Bangkok.

After ten days in Bangkok, Linda and I need a break from our tight publicity schedule. Linda has booked a flight to the Island of Phuket, off the west coast of the Thai peninsula in the Andaman Sea. This will be a restful pause for two exhausted ladies, looking forward to incognito relaxation after non-stop public exposure.

October 16-19, Wednesday through Saturday

Wednesday morning, Linda and I catch the van to the airport and fly to Phuket for our welcome rest. The resort is reminiscent of a Caribbean Island or a village on the Mexican Riviera. It is third-world and plain, with scattered areas of gorgeous beach and luxury hotels. Our hotel, the Katathani, is at Kata Beach on the far southwest quarter of the island, some distance from town. It's nice, but basic—a "Holiday Inn, compared to the Shangri-La," as Linda describes it. But it is exactly right for us.

The pristine beach forms a graceful curve between two protective promontories, like bookends for the bay. Private and quiet, it offers gorgeous surf and warm, inviting water. The water temperature is about 80 degrees and the air about 95. Periodic rain showers feel cool and clean. There are very few beach vendors (they are discouraged by the management) and little commercial development outside the hotel. From our balcony, we have a centered view of the bay and beach, with tranquil gardens between.

Besides its serene setting, we discover other advantages. The resort has three lovely swimming pools with massage available on the beach and poolside. No noisy night life disturbs the quiet, and the food here is good. We especially like the seafood restaurant, perfect for open-air sunset suppers. There, Linda can also enjoy her new favorite drink, watermelon daiquiris.

Speaking practically, there are two other benefits. We have Internet access for our ongoing communication with family, despite feeling as if we're on the edge of the earth. It's also economical. Here, we're saving enough over the much higher cost of the Shangri-La to cover the cost of our extra travel.

The first full day we dedicated to rest—the sun, sand, surf, pool, Singha beer, and naps. This second day we feel more active. After luxuriating with Thai massages on the beach, we set out to explore the island. I had always dreamed of riding an elephant, and this is the place! Siam Safari provides a trek by elephant through the jungle, with mountaintop views of the coastline. This is exactly what Linda and I sought. Riding on the gentle creatures' undulating backs, I can touch their leathery skin and take photos of young elephant working with their trainers.

The trainers (*mahouts)* are at one with these massive animals. They ride on the elephants' heads and communicate with bare feet gently prodding the backs of the animals' ears. They encourage, urge, and chastise their giant friends through soft grunts and Thai words. Until I climbed on an elephant's back, I never knew how small we humans are beside these behemoths. But I love the feel of my elephant's shoulder and her inch-thick skin under my bare feet. I'm fascinated by the trainer's gentle toe touches to urge her on, especially when the trail goes downhill (probably fearsome for her). My giant is thirty-five years old, turning pink in spots—a sign of elephant aging. As we rock along, the mahout points out rubber trees lining the trail. We can reach out and pull pure, raw rubber from the closest one. These fresh pieces stretch greatly and smell exactly like new latex gloves.

After our elephant trek, our driver takes us around the island. In Phuket Town, we shop for native Thai goods—a skirt and scarf for me, beads and bracelet for Linda. Then we drive past Patong Beach, a swinging place for the young, wannabe young, gay, and thrill-seeking folks. It's like Waikiki or Coney Island: fast food and myriad shops, hundreds of tuk-tuks, taxis, rude drivers, and air pollution. It is everything I hate about most resorts. Moreover, not one hotel actually sits on the beach. All this chaos separates tourist lodgings from the sea. Seeing the contrast makes us even happier with our quiet refuge at Katathani. This short vacation in Phuket will be a shining ornament in our Thailand memories.

We pack up early the following day to return to Bangkok. After an uneventful flight, we hurry to the Shangri-La to swim and relax. Wrapped in towels, we order supper by the pool. Linda has her "last watermelon daiquiri"—at least for this trip. I'm relieved that no one, except poor Paul, got sick during our stay in Thailand. Linda and I half expected "Bali Belly," the usual diarrhea from impure water and iffy food, but we both stayed entirely well. I could concentrate on my work here with no health worries. I'm also grateful for the safe environment and blessed quiet of this lovely hotel, our haven in the midst of the madness of the streets.

October 20, Sunday, our last day in Bangkok

My final engagement is a book signing on the closing day of the Expo. We take a taxi to the Queen Sirikit National Conference Center and find our way to the Se-Ed booth. Arriving early, I go straight to work inscribing people's books. The heaviest traffic day of the book fair is usually now, at the end.

An elderly Japanese man is my most memorable customer. He speaks rapidly, looking first at me and then at his translator. He's very animated. At first, his spirited tirade appears to be a rant about homosexuality. Finally, I see his point. His daughter is a "Tom," a lesbian, and he's confused and disappointed and sad. His worry is familiar: he needs to know "if it is the parents' fault." He wonders if I think the gay person can change. I hate to dash his hope for that but must answer truthfully. By the end of our conversation, his defeated face is heart-wrenching. Clearly, I'm involved with a worldwide sadness that straight spouses and parents share. Life is not easy anywhere.

At 12:30, the book signing session ends. Linda and I make our way to the Debut Café to meet Boom. Paul, barely out of the hospital, is already here with Yord and five of their gay guy friends. Boom hurries in, along with Sarawanee and a couple of others. Boom is elated that her mid-term exams are finished. We're all primed for a celebration! For our final lunch together, Sarawanee offers gifts—beautiful scarves and CDs of the Thai king's music. I'm surely the most fortunate American in Thailand, blessed with this tight network of wonderful new friends. Every time we encountered an obstacle, in transportation or scheduling or special skills required, one of these people stepped in. Most endearing is Boom's bond with Yord—"best girlfriends." It's a lovely thing to watch.

When it's almost time to leave, one of Sarawanee's friends rushes up to the table, bringing a copy of my book to sign. She offers her business card "to stay in touch." As she hands it to me, I admire her polished silver card holder—and she promptly gives it to me to keep. Such gift-giving has been a hallmark of this whole trip. Generosity of spirit characterizes the Thai people.

Suddenly Phra Chai appears. Once again, he's traveled for hours to meet us, compelled by a mission. He wants me to carry a letter to my gay husband's mother. He digs in his bag to find something to write on. Pulling out an envelope and an old flyer, he carefully prints his message in his rudimentary English:

To Margaret: a far away letter from Asia.

Here I am Chai, a gay monk from Thailand. I'd like to tell you please accept your son, Jim. Homosexul is normal. There are we all around the world. The good thing from mother is to love son fully.

METTA, CHAI

How fitting that Phra Chai signed his letter to Margaret, *Metta, Chai. Metta* means lovingkindness or universal friendliness. That is what Phra Chai longs for from his own family, and what we all need.

Looking back at the unexpected, dramatic events of these past two decades, I'm convinced that I am living my karma: my experience-teachers manifested into a clear vocation of writing to heal. Working with straight spouses utilizes all my accumulated skills—teaching, listening, speaking, and particularly writing. It has provided a clear sense of purpose and a brief taste of fame in this exotic country. The result is the path.

A Tale of Two Marriages

FOR THREE YEARS AFTER OUR COURTSHIP BEGAN IN England, Dale and I were practically inseparable. Chester had been enchanting, so we continued to see each other and travel together at every opportunity. We shared a transatlantic cruise and an extended trip to Australia during that time. We snowshoed at Brainard Lake in our nearby mountains and enjoyed season tickets to the Boulder Philharmonic and dinner theater. Our adventures in far-flung places offered mutual memories, while quiet times at home drew us even closer. Having felt so disoriented after my divorce from Jim, I was eager to regain the security of a committed relationship. Perhaps too eager.

November 27, 1999

On a cold and sunny boulder day, dale and I were formally married in victorian style—lacy, cream-colored wedding dress, flowers and boutonnieres, family and friends to witness, wedding cake, and a champagne reception. It was a storybook beginning for a new life for both of us. It felt right to make our relationship official, and our sweet, old-fashioned wedding appeared flawless, just as i'd dreamed it would be. That's how it seems, when one is unwilling to look beyond the surface. Through our courtship, I chose to ignore dale's sometimes erratic actions, remolding reality into an idealized package. I wanted it so badly.

It was naïve. Even on our wedding night, Dale opened yet another bottle of champagne in our hotel room—and drank it. This was the crack in our relationship that widened with time. Serene, then stormy. Up, then down. Talkative, then silent. Jekyll, then Hyde. What would any new day bring? Ecstasy or explosion?

As months passed, Dale spent more and more time away from home. He taught his classes at the university but spent afternoons in his familiar bars or having long cocktail hours at a buddy's home. Sometimes our love for each other was clear and pure and exciting, but I was often home alone with growing apprehension.

Soon, the root of my husband's frequent moodiness and outbursts was indisputable. Dale's habitually late arrivals home and unpredictable mood swings revealed a problem that we both wanted to deny. He was an alcoholic, and his disease was progressing.

An accidental fall on his drinking friend's icy driveway led to a pivotal crisis. Dale's leg was fractured, but he refused to seek treatment at first, self-medicating with vodka. By the time the break was medically diagnosed, it required delicate surgery and pins, which led to a life-threatening sepsis infection.

Seriously ill, he was bedridden, on heavy medication for months. I was homebound as his caregiver, and it was grueling for both us. Through this whole episode, Dale found ways to drink in secret, filling empty liquor bottles with water to avoid detection. He eventually recuperated from his terrible infection, but his distance and dark moods continued. Denial of his addiction became impossible.

We reached a crisis just sixteen months after our wedding. Late one evening, I was in our narrow, walk-in closet, talking on my cell phone with a straight spouse who needed counsel. Dale came through the back door, drunk, calling me. When I didn't immediately respond, he kept raising his voice.

"I'm on the phone!" I exclaimed.

His angry voice grew louder as he raged into the bedroom, my friend on the phone hearing it all. I hastily hung up, but Dale kept bellowing that I wasn't listening, that I wasn't paying attention to him. He stood, livid, blocking the door of the closet, waving his arms and yelling. There was no reasoning with him, and I was scared!

Slowly, I walked toward him, and he stumbled back from the door, opening space for me to breathe—and escape. I had no idea what had triggered his illogical fury, but I had seen too much of it. Still incoherently angry, he grabbed his car keys, slammed through the front door, and drove away.

Bolting the door behind him, I made a hard decision. "This is enough. I'm through." With new energy and absolute determination, I gathered up everything that belonged to Dale, including his billfold, which he had left behind in his haste. Though we were living there, he had never completely moved into my house. His clothes and other belongings all fit into two large black garbage bags. A fitting container, I thought.

At dawn the next morning, I nervously drove into Dale's driveway. I knew he'd still be sleeping. Lurking like a thief, I unloaded the two bags and leaned them against his garage door.

With a sad sigh, I drove home and again bolted the door. That was the end of our "storybook" marriage.

Dale's descent into alcoholism progressed apace, especially after I filed for divorce. Our abrupt separation drove him even further into depression and addiction. I was afraid for him but more afraid of a future with him. Once again, it took a life-threatening accident to force a change of direction.

Returning from a grueling trip to attend separate professional board meetings in three separate countries, Dale returned to Denver. He arrived at the airport so inebriated that he stumbled and fell all the way down a long, narrow escalator. Bleeding from a bad cut on his head, barely conscious, he was taken to the airport's first aid station. Heidi, a graduate student who had come to drive him home, responded to an airport page and found Dale in dire need of medical attention with a probable concussion. She wanted to take him straight to the hospital, but Dale doggedly insisted that she take him home instead. There was no reasoning with him, so she bowed to his request. Just as she was about to leave his house, Dale fell down again, cutting another gash in his head. This time, Heidi drove him to the emergency room.

"We don't want you to die!" Heidi pleaded, standing over him in the hospital. Michael, her fellow PhD student, who had been living in a rented a room at Dale's house, was there to back her up. Propped up in his hospital bed, now confronted by his two most valued doctoral students, Dale finally faced his addiction, this demon that had nearly killed him. Gambling their own academic futures by challenging their major professor, the two courageous young people convinced him that he must accept treatment in order to survive.

They had planned well. With the counsel of Dale's closest friend, a professor at an eastern university, they had previously researched and selected a respected recovery center in California. They reserved a place there for Dale, and Michael was prepared to accompany him on the flight and admit him to the clinic for a thirty-day residential program. Finally persuaded by their caring insistence, Dale handed them his credit card and acquiesced. He would accept treatment.

Suffering from his severe injuries and the rigors of detox, Dale was at first bedridden at the clinic. But the clinic's expert care was transformational. One month later, still recovering from his concussion and other wounds, weakened by years of alcohol abuse, shaky physically, but imbued with new self-knowledge, he emerged from treatment, determined to get well. He knew he had to reinvent himself and his way of life. It was a fresh start.

Back in Boulder, Dale laid out a program to continue his recovery. He exercised regularly at the YMCA, attended daily meetings of Alcoholics Anonymous, virtually memorized Bill W's "Big Book," and practiced the Twelve Steps religiously. He was saving his own life, hoping for a new beginning with me.

The first time I saw Dale after his return from California, I watched him cross the parking lot at the Y, carrying his gym bag and looking quite pale and thin. I ducked behind a parked car to avoid a meeting. (When we last spoke, he had been furious with me. That was the day I had essentially forced him to sign our divorce papers, threatening to have them served by the sheriff.) There in the public parking lot, I needn't have been afraid. He didn't want to blame me—he hoped we could reconcile.

Shortly after coming back to Boulder, he initiated many attempts to "make amends," following AA's Ninth Step directive. I rebuffed him at first, but he tenaciously persisted. Almost daily, he brought a note or card to my house, filled with shaky, handwritten messages of love. Despite my doubts, my protests didn't deter him. He was determined.

I struggled to keep my distance, even as Dale slowly improved his health and self-knowledge through AA. I had worked hard to accept my circumstances as a single woman—again—and I avoided any thought of reconciliation. I maintained my own home and traveled alone and with friends. Civic responsibilities also filled my days—president of Boulder Rotary, another term on the Naropa University Board. I became certified as a fitness instructor at the Y and taught classes there, also giving Watsu treatments in my home pool. In between, I practiced meditation and spent hours at my desk, writing—always writing. My drive to live a satisfying life *on my own* was almost manic.

My first book, *My Husband Is Gay,* had recently been published, so I was still immersed in publicity efforts, busy with radio and television interviews, developing a niche market. Still, nights were lonely. I enrolled in a divorce recovery seminar and went back into therapy, doggedly determined to solidify my independent path. Through it all, Dale continued to call me and send artistic cards that declared his devotion, each one a reminder of what we had lost.

Around 2002, Dale's name slowly reappeared in my calendar book: "Cookout at Dale's," "Lunch at Sawaddee's, Dale," "Dinner at John's, Dale," "Take Dale to DIA for flight to Morocco." My fear and resistance were breaking down. Tender feelings and hope rekindled, as Dale maintained his sobriety. Carefully retaining relative independence, we drew closer to a reunion, though another drastic change with uncertain consequence lay ahead. Dale was approaching retirement from the university. His thirty-year teaching career there would end in 2004, though his international work with entrepreneurs would continue for several more years.

By 2005, Dale was steadfast in his sobriety, actively sponsoring others in AA, and imbued with a desire to "give back" and help others. He was better than ever, and my trust was restored. We had a future together again. We made plans to downsize from my Treehouse and refurbish his home at Bluebell. We also envisioned another wedding, a simple commitment ceremony in the Buddhist tradition. When Treehouse finally sold, after a tense eight months in a declining real estate market, Dale and I were well into our extensive remodel of Bluebell.

Simplifying our residence was symbolic of our evolving lifestyle. Our renewed connection reflected spiritual changes. Sentimentally, we set our new wedding date for the same day as our first one, November 27. This time, instead of an utterly traditional, American ceremony, we would have a Mahayana Buddhist rite, based on the bodhisattva ideals of exchanging self for other, practicing generosity, discipline, patience, exertion, meditation, and wisdom. Our vows would reflect a commitment to these ideals and to each other. My meditation instructor, Acharya Dale Asrael, agreed to be the Preceptor, and my therapist and canoe buddy, Dr. Deborah Bowman, was the Shrine Keeper. Our ceremony would take place in the spacious upstairs study in our renewed Bluebell home. It would be an intimate service, with only our closest friends present as witnesses.

In the fall, when we planned our wedding, construction at Bluebell was on schedule. Then a hard winter hit early. It was particularly snowy, causing long construction delays. As our special day neared, the unfinished house was still cluttered with lumber and power saws and tool boxes on the main floor. My study was almost finished but still covered with construction dust, and there was no electrical power. With wedding invitations already mailed and arrangements in place for a celebratory supper afterward, we determined to ignore the construction and carry out the whole original plan. The day before the ceremony, friends helped get the space adequately clean, and we carried folding chairs up the stairs. We placed candles around the room in all the window sills to provide soft light, and Deborah improvised a shrine. I had ethereal Ikebana flower arrangements delivered the following morning to provide freshness and cheer. The setting was perfect in its imperfection.

November 27, 2006

Surrounded by loving friends and flickering candlelight, precisely seven years after our first wedding, Dale and I committed the rest of our lives to each other, this time in a lasting spiritual bond and wiser love.

Sense of Place

NO ONE COULD HAVE HAD A MORE SECURE UPBRINGING than I. An only child in a devoted family, I was safe and protected in the solid rock home that my dad built on West 8th Street in Tulsa. My parents were married in the living room of that house, operated their business from there, and thrived in that home until they sold their trucking company and retired decades later. It was a center of cooperative hard work, harmony, and unconditional love. It was my innocent refuge and place of complete acceptance from the time I was born until I left for college. Growing up there, my home was essential to my sense of self, and I learned to sink deep roots in my later places of residence.

Household moves require taking stock, weeding out unimportant possessions, paring down, taking risks, and making a leap into the unknown. Apprehension is predictable, topped by heady excitement. In my experience, each move to a different city also carried some unexpected spiritual impact, not fully evident until later. In Buddhist terms, my physical relocations now appear to be "karmic seeds ripening." Each fresh setting opened unanticipated causes and effects that became clear only in hindsight.

As newlyweds, Jim and I moved five times. Each new place revealed a different slant on our personal relationship and our future professions. We relocated from Enid, Oklahoma, to Plainview and then Fort Worth, Texas, back to Tulsa, Oklahoma, and finally to Portland, Oregon—all within our first eighteen months together.

After graduation from Phillips University in Enid, our first brief landing was in west Texas, where Jim had a summer job as youth minister at the Plainview Christian Church. There was a small Baptist college in town where I completed one last required class for certification to teach in Texas. In late August, we moved into married student housing in Fort Worth for Jim's graduate studies at Texas Christian University and my first full-time teaching job at Arlington Heights High School. Such frequent moves were predictable for a young couple just starting married life, but our subsequent changes of residence were different, each precipitated by some apparent coincidence that led to a major turning point.

Karmic Seeds Ripening

Looking back, these significant household moves were a study in flukes—accidents that opened surprising opportunities. The first example occurred in Fort Worth. In December 1961, I became pregnant during my first year of teaching. To my dismay, Fort Worth schools released teachers from the classroom after their pregnancies "showed." Without recourse, I lost my job and our sole source of income at Easter time. With uncertain finances, we left TCU and Fort Worth in June and moved to Tulsa to be near family and to welcome Stephen, our first child, born in September. None of this was planned in advance.

Almost immediately, Jim found a good job with Shell Oil, but after only five months in Tulsa, there was another fluke—an unexpected phone call from Portland. One of Jim's former class-mates from TCU had landed the position of associate minister at the largest Christian Church in Oregon. He recommended Jim as a candidate for their new church business administrator. The job matched Jim's academic training and chosen career goal, so he was thrilled at the prospect. As he interviewed, I tried to imagine how I could possibly cope with a three-month-old baby that far away from family and familiar surroundings. Despite my apprehension, Jim accepted the church's offer. With consid-erable anxiety, we drove our packed car to Oregon. (I learned only decades later that Jim's TCU friend was also gay and intro-duced him to that side of life in our new hometown.)

We settled into a little house in a suburb of Portland. I soon found sporadic work as a substitute teacher, engaging a lovely, grandmotherly lady who could come to our home to take care of Stephen. The principal of Sunset High School, where I occa-sionally taught, recommended me for a temporary assignment to teach seventh grade English at an exclusive boys' boarding school. Their regular teacher was recovering from emergency surgery. My appointment at Bishop Dagwell Hall was obviously not planned; the administration's offer rose out of desperation. I was the only female teacher on their large male faculty, and I "mothered" twenty little seventh graders during their first lonely year at boarding school.

Success in that temporary position made way for a similar assignment, this time to substitute for an ailing professor at Pacific University in nearby Forest Grove. I commuted three days a week to teach two sections of freshman English there. By the end of that semester, I had a new career goal—to teach in college. I immediately enrolled in graduate school at Pacific, and my professional objective was clear. Were these just accidents? I sought none of these fortunate engagements. Each turn of events was an unanticipated opportunity.

Jim and I had been in Portland for four years and our family had grown to four by the time I finished my master's degree with distinction. Our younger son, Gary, was born halfway through my graduate program. He was just eighteen months old when the next windfall came to our family. The dean of Phillips University unexpectedly visited us in Portland the summer of 1966. He had come in person to offer Jim a position as director of university relations back in Enid. As we continued our conversation that day, the dean learned of my new degree from Pacific. Almost as an afterthought, he spoke of an opening for a "one-semester" temporary slot in their Department of English, again to substitute for an incapacitated professor. Would I be interested?

The prospect of returning to our beloved alma mater was compelling for both Jim and me. With great excitement, we sold our home and moved again in August from rainy Portland back to familiar Oklahoma. Back at Phillips, my one-semester appointment was extended into a rewarding seven-year position, promotion to assistant professor, and being honored as Teacher of the Year in 1972. Once again, I was an anomaly in a male-dominated environment, one of just three women on a faculty of eighty, and my original job offer was "coincidental."

After six years in Enid, a family vacation to Colorado led to the next life-changing fluke. A fiery kitchen accident at Phillips University Science Camp put the camp cook in the hospital and left sixty hungry students and faculty with no one to prepare meals. That emergency precipitated my impulsive offer to stay on as the camp cook. Our planned family weekend morphed into an insanely difficult and rewarding summer job in the wilds of Colorado. Enchanted by the river and evergreen forests and high-altitude climate, I developed a passion for the mountains, and my life direction shifted once more.

The following year, after marital tumult and near-divorce, Jim and I recommitted for a fresh start in those mountains. During spring break in 1973, we "shopped" for a new place to live, driving from Albuquerque up the front range of the Colorado Rockies, as far north as Fort Collins. As we drove through each town, we wondered, "How would it feel to live here? What could we do to make a living?"

Colorado Springs seemed a possibility, until we passed through Denver and drove over the top of Davidson Mesa. From a rest stop on the mesa, we surveyed a town nestled in a green valley with the vast expanse of the Rocky Mountains as a backdrop. It took my breath away. Boulder was the place. Exploring job possibilities there, we searched the want ads and found nothing. We soon realized that our church and academic work history was not conducive to regular employment outside those fields.

Then we resorted to a small employment agency, Acme Personnel Service. It was a one-person operation. Once again, we stumbled onto opportunity. When the owner shook his head helplessly as he reviewed our resumes, Jim inquired about the prospects for buying some existing small business, perhaps a print shop or other such service. "Do you know of any for sale?" he asked. "This one is!" the owner exclaimed.

How hard could this be? He had phones, *Yellow Pages* ads, pleasantly furnished offices in a professional downtown building. There were files of applicants and a franchise organization to give us initial training. After quick research, we made an offer for the elegant sum of $9,000, and we were suddenly in business. We resigned from Phillips, sold our home for seed money, and claimed our mountains.

Above all others, this particular relocation was a significant turning point. In the hippie days of 1973, Boulder presented a totally different environment, much more diverse and edgy than Oklahoma. Our sons felt uprooted at first, less enthusiastic than I'd hoped. Steve, especially, longed for his friends and our old life in Enid. It didn't help that we had a frightening experience our first week in Boulder. Shopping for school supplies at the Ben Franklin store near our apartment, we witnessed a shoplifter running through the aisle, the manager close behind, yelling "Stop, thief!" Steve looked at me pleadingly and said, "I want to move back to Enid." It was a rough beginning.

Our choice to settle in liberal Boulder, rather than conservative Colorado Springs, also made an enormous difference. This university town was a brash new frontier in the seventies, open to newcomers and innovation. Despite one serious economic downturn that pushed us to the brink, we remained determined to grow our business. We expanded our permanent employment placements to include temporary help. Offering that new service gave us a competitive edge with unforeseen potential. With a supportive business climate and years of committed teamwork, we grew our mom-and-pop start-up into a multi-office national staffing industry leader. Jim and I labored side by side for twenty-three years to achieve that success. Our effort ensured financial security, even after our eventual divorce.

Boulder is also a hotbed of philosophical alternatives. For me, it has been a spiritual feast. It unlocked my philosophical evolution in unimagined directions. For that reason alone, our move to Boulder was a pivotal decision of this lifetime.

Coming Home

Between 1962, when Jim and I lived in Tulsa for six short months, and 1988, we bought four homes—in Tulsa, Portland, Enid, and the Edinboro Drive place in Boulder. All were comfortable and welcoming, but I didn't connect with those houses in an intimate way. Both Jim and I were too immersed during those years in bringing up our two lively sons and building our corporation. By 1988, we had been married for twenty-six years, our boys were both high school graduates, launched into out-of-state colleges, and our staffing company was hugely successful. We decided to look for a new home that better suited our changing lifestyle and tastes. I found Treehouse.

Treehouse was the first home I ever *named*. When I first walked through the front door with the realtor, I was surrounded by an elusive woodsy scent. This warm house was lovingly built of fine, fragrant woods. The living room walls were solid red oak, the floor a dark exotic wood called apitong. The master bedroom walls were rich American red cherry. Even the vaulted ceilings were golden pine. Built on a sloping lot, the main living area was on the second-floor level, with an indoor swimming pool and guest suite below. Huge windows overlooked a terraced, park-like yard, filled with Austrian pine, Colorado blue spruce, linden, ancient cottonwoods, fruit trees, and mountain ash. Adjacent to a steep, undeveloped hillside, it emulated mountain living in the heart of town. The place sang to me and felt like a living presence. Here, I could sink deep roots once again. I was fortunate to feel so embraced by this place, for only three years later, sitting in that very garden, Jim would come out and change our lives completely.

From the beginning, Treehouse was a spiritual place for me. It had a tangible character. After Jim came out and moved away, I remained there to fashion a new way of life. The house was my rock in those next few years. The warm indoor swimming pool became my Watsu practice center. A new writing studio was carved from the space that had once been a tool-filled workshop off the garage. There, I produced my first two books and toiled as chair of the Naropa University Trustees and president of Boulder Rotary. Treehouse was home base when I launched the book tour that took me to faraway Thailand. It was the scene of multiple television and radio interviews. Many group canoeing adventures were organized there, and it provided gracious housing for my cherished Buddhist teacher on one memorable occasion.

Treehouse represents a major segment of my long life. In my eighteen years there, that home witnessed my evolution of self-awareness. While it sheltered fierce competitive striving for professional recognition, civic leadership, and outdoor expertise, it also provided a place to rest from incessant public demands. Its expansive grounds encouraged gardening mastery. Those Treehouse years even brought a small measure of fame as an author. Always stretching beyond my strength, I could return for rest in this place I loved. At Treehouse, I learned how to live an independent, self-sufficient, single life.

It took some major upheavals to pry me out of Treehouse, though the upkeep of such a large home had become difficult. My next turning point was falling in love again and beginning a new phase of life, marrying Dale for the second time. Together, we transformed his home of thirty-five years from an aging bungalow to an updated traditional home for the two of us. His original house was built in 1906, one of only four homes in the entire area. At that time, it was a chicken farm, south of the city limits of Boulder. The family who owned it supplied eggs and chickens to the famous Brown Palace Hotel in Denver. Now, this renewed home is nestled in a quiet, established neighborhood, remodeled and surrounded by flower gardens. We named it Bluebell. It fits, because gardening is a special pleasure for both Dale and me.

Bluebell has become as dear to me as Treehouse, and it also holds reminders of my childhood home. The original house had the same floorplan as my folks'—an entry porch, combined living-dining room, and the kitchen at the back. Two small bedrooms off the living room were connected by a hallway and bath. When Dale and I remodeled his place, we protected the integrity of the exterior turn-of-the-century design and built our new space unobtrusively on the back. Our remodel added a master suite, laundry room, double garage, back deck, finished basement, and a spacious upstairs study for me. My sunny studio is a spiritual and creative refuge and was the setting for our Buddhist wedding ceremony. Windows on all sides look out on aspen and pine, with a close-up view west to the front range of the Rockies. This tranquil space fosters focused writing at my desk or contemplation in a meditation corner. A wall of bookshelves houses my library, and comfortable seating welcomes our weekly dharma study group.

While all of my family's residences were peaceful and inviting, it's clear that these last two "named" homes offered much more than an address. Treehouse and Bluebell have both provided a serene sense of place where emotional and spiritual roots grow deep and where the home itself is like family.

Karmic Choices

Any summary of symbolic household moves is a mere outline of decades of action and growth. It is like an X-ray of my life, seeing through flesh and blood to the bare skeleton. A chronological description is as sterile as that X-ray. These homes all throbbed with daily events that overflowed with anticipation and disappointment, praise and blame, revelation and tears, ambition and tragedy—the achievements and defeats that fuel human experience. These bare bones gain flesh and breath only through the stories I tell myself, inventions of belief, and memories that are the beating heart and pulse of life.

Still, even this abbreviated history reveals a striking number of apparent accidents—amazing coincidences. In the belief system of my childhood, I would have attributed these unexpected turns to God's plan for my life—divine guidance. While that may be true, I'm more inclined to describe these pivotal flukes as opportunities seized in a spirit of adventure. Or perhaps they are karmic choices, recognized through a conscious life.

Passageway

I stand at the door,
Eastern sun pouring
gold on a garden
of numinous delight.
Every flower of earth
invites my gaze.
Awed and still,
I feast on their beauty,
fascinated, as one by one
flowers come to me,
mystically float past
into shaded space behind me.
As they pass my threshold
I touch velvet petals
marvel at matchless hues
see each as unique.
I welcome every bloom
anticipate the next
and the next.

Behind me
light from the doorway
fades into dark.
I don't look back.
I stand always
on this threshold

awake in this dream
as my future
passes into my past.

Spiritual Odyssey

Faith of Origin

I DIDN'T DARE LOOK AT THE SHADOWED, SMILING FACES IN the rows behind my mother. I was all alone up front in the quiet sanctuary. A holiday wreath decorated the pulpit, and a traditional manger scene was arranged nearby. Facing the Sunday night crowd in the cozy warmth of Westside Christian Church, I focused my gaze on Mama's slight form, leaning toward me from the front row. I felt a little anxious, and I stroked the soft folds of my new navy velvet dress that Mama had sewn for me the week before. She held a children's book in her hands and nodded reassurance as I kept my eyes on her face and began.

'Twas the night before Christmas, when all through the house
Not a creature was stirring, not even a mouse. ...

I must have been only three or four in this earliest pre-school memory of the church my family attended then. My parents weren't active in the church, but "Mother May," my paternal grandmother who lived next door to us, made sure that I went to Sunday School regularly, along with my three orphaned cousins who lived with her. I remember standing beside her on the seat of our pew, holding a hymnal during congregational singing, even before I could read the words. I can still hear her wavering alto voice etched in memory, singing "In the Garden," her favorite hymn. *I come to the garden alone, / While the dew is still on the roses.* ... Later, when Mother May transferred her membership to the larger congregation at First Christian in Sand Springs, my cousins and I continued to attend church with her.

Church camp highlighted each summer from seventh grade on. I was baptized by immersion when I turned twelve. By ninth grade, I was fully engaged at First Christian, playing piano for the first grade Sunday School class, singing in the choir, and enjoying Sunday night fun with my best friends in the youth group. That's where I first met Jim, my future husband, whose family had recently relocated to Sand Springs from Texas. This church was the core of my social life growing up, particularly after Jim and I began dating, when I was just sixteen, a high school sophomore. Attending Phillips University, a Christian Church-affiliated college deepened my commitment to that denomination's belief system. The January before our college graduation, Jim and I were married in a traditional, formal ceremony at University Place Christian Church.

Through our five household moves during the next eventful year, the church remained a central influence. Jim's first job after graduation from Phillips was as the youth minister at his family's home church in west Texas. After that summer job, he enrolled at Texas Christian University in Fort Worth for graduate studies, and his first real career position was business administrator for the leading Christian Church in the state of

Oregon. Clearly, our devout belief was the foundation for both personal and professional decisions.

Living in liberal Oregon, far away from Bible Belt attitudes and culture, I began to doubt some of the conservative religious assumptions of my youth. Jim's work at a venerable downtown institution was also replete with "high church" formalities and expectations, foreign to this small-town newcomer. At the uncertain age of twenty-three, my role was essentially that of a minister's wife—an unpaid adjunct to my husband's position. I was additionally challenged by the demands of mothering an infant, teaching, and beginning graduate school at Pacific University. When our second son, Gary, was born December 18, 1964, I was still in school, drowning in responsibility, and emotionally and physically overwhelmed. Where was the security of my childhood faith?

Our opportunity to move back to Enid with two sudden, unsolicited job offers at Phillips presented an escape for me. We returned to familiar surroundings with slightly greater financial security from two salaries. Teaching at that level was very demanding, but my confidence grew each year. At the same time, active involvement in a progressive congregation at Enid's Church of the Covenant anchored our family life.

Our return to Enid was in 1966, during the tumultuous era of the Vietnam War, widespread protest, Woodstock, flower children, and free love. Joining a very liberal church and connecting with other young faculty friends opened a different kind of social community. Experimentation was encouraged and expected, social norms loosened. Jim and I soon slipped into a party-loving circle of couples who became intimate friends. Our formerly staid and sober social life was history. Weekends usually offered a welcome break from the intellectual demands of our work with alcohol-infused merriment and a release of pious prohibitions.

Catalyst for Change

After six years in Enid, my accidental job as the camp cook at the Phillips Science Camp was another spiritual turning point. From our first night at the camp, visiting our friends' log cabin, warmed by a wood stove, with our children around us, I felt oddly at home. Fragrant pines, the whirr of hummingbirds, and the soft murmur of the river filled me with unfamiliar peace. The very next day, the camp cook's fateful accident allowed me to remain in Colorado and deepen my connection with the land. I worked in the kitchen for the rest of the summer. Jim returned to Enid with Steve, who was playing Little League baseball that year, and Gary stayed with me to explore his own mountain adventures.

Those weeks at camp were both heaven and hell. Even with two student helpers in the kitchen, it was grueling physical work to plan and prepare three meals a day for sixty people, six days a week. But my difficulties were offset by rushes of near ecstasy. I fell in love in a new way, drawing nature into my heart with grateful awe and creating poems like "Camera" that remain as keen reminders of this vital turning point. I lost fourteen pounds from sheer exertion, but at night I sang my heart's song in those mountains. When the academic term ended in August, it was bittersweet to return to ordinary routines in Oklahoma.

Camera

How shall I save
these spots of time
to ungloom winter?
Can I leaf through thought
to live again
pictures I love most?

Translucent half-moon
caught on piney hilltop,
snow-shower whitening
bones of an old boomtown
cabins intact, though lives,
loves within are gone.
Rain touching my face
with green breeze
and deep-down freshness.
Tree-roof overhead,
mossy shelter
to ease a storm.
A doe
frightened out of sight
and hundreds of wildflowers
framing an aspen lake.
A waterfall picnic
one tiny mauve blossom
unique in all the world.
A broken stone,
its special shape

my keepsake.
River sound at night
and rain on the roof
while woodsmoke
cozies a cabin.
Wading an icy stream
to marvel at sunlight shimmer
through rain-studded pines.
Reading on the swinging bridge,
my chipmunk friend
visiting at twilight—
and spruce smell always.

My camera worked long
to snap sensuous moments,
vivid and sweet.
Enjoy the delights
of this memory album.
It belongs to you as well.

I returned to Science Camp the following summer, this time as an instructor of writing and poetry. The second trip there substantiated my heart's connection with the Colorado mountains. By this time, Jim and I had worked at Phillips for seven years and were increasingly restless. Our marriage was strained to the breaking point already, and long-term career prospects were limited at the university. We reluctantly agreed that it was time to leave academia, make a new start, and try to mend our marriage. We gave up our positions at Phillips and headed west.

Staking our precarious future on the failing employment agency we bought, we made a new start in Boulder. We were financially and emotionally strapped at the time. Fortunately, our former pattern of church involvement provided a familiar haven during the insane amount of work of those first few years in business. Boulder's First Christian Church became our refuge. Our two sons were baptized there when the time was right, and I sponsored the youth group and later became a deacon, then an elder. Our social activities again involved party-loving church friends, though we were most often engulfed by the stressful demands of our fledgling business. Working together with common goals drew the two of us closer again. We were a good team with complementary skills, and our company thrived.

During all these changes, my Christian faith was the foundation of my spiritual life. From early childhood through parenthood and young adulthood, I had accepted the traditional teachings without challenge. Fervent and unquestioning, I possessed what Buddhist author Sharon Salzberg called "Bright Faith" in her book *Faith: Trusting Your Own Deepest Experience*. As a protégé of the Oklahoma Bible Belt environment, I had remained a true believer through our many household moves and recurring marital uncertainties. My faith seemed unshakable.

Spiritual Confusion

By the mid-eighties, both of our sons had graduated high school and were immersed in their university studies out of state. Our business was flourishing, having grown from a mom-and-pop start-up to a multi-office, cutting-edge staffing company involving two separate corporations. Jim and I were building a fortune and living high. We traveled frequently, enjoyed multiple cruises all over the world, owned a luxury house boat on Lake Powell, and were known in Boulder for a glittering social life.

Despite outer appearances, I experienced growing spiritual dissatisfaction. Something essential was lacking. Perhaps the culprit was menopause or boredom with repetitive sermons. No longer inspired, I drifted away from the church, questioning it all. If the Bible is infallible truth, why are there so many inconsistencies, and why have people through the ages used these same stories to justify their bloody wars? Doubts about my religion were pushed to action by a hurtful rift with the minister's wife. I decided to leave First Christian altogether and try something different. For a few months, I attended a Methodist church, but it seemed repetitious, more conservative, and even less satisfying.

A newspaper article about the Unity Church of Boulder caught my attention, and I visited services there, enjoying its openness and fresh outlook. Humanistic messages and the Peace Song at the end of each service touched me deeply. It was there that I had my first taste of meditation. It was lightweight, only a few minutes at a time, often with background music or spoken guidance, but it did allay some restlessness. I was on to something different that felt more satisfying than wearisome platitudes. I wanted to go deeper into silence.

Drawing on Boulder's rich environment for experimental spirituality, I explored the Buddhist programs at Naropa and Karma Dzong, the downtown temple. Tapping into those resources, I plunged into focused study of the Shambhala tradition in books by Ani Pema Chödrön. I practiced sitting meditation in frequent weekend retreats and on the Naropa campus with my meditation instructor, Acharya Dale Asrael. I was captivated by this exotic Buddhist island in the center of my adopted hometown. It was utterly foreign to all my previous experience, but it was uniquely comforting. More and more, I enjoyed sitting in the Naropa meditation hall, surrounded by the fragrance of incense, soothed by serene silence.

By 1991, as my spiritual life grew richer, my personal life was deteriorating. When Jim came out that May, I gradually realized the extent of my dilemma. I learned more of his double life as a gay man, his hundreds of anonymous sexual encounters over twenty-five years, and I saw that our comfortable life together was irretrievable. It took nearly four more tumultuous years to accomplish our separation. Until the sale of our business, we had to maintain a public pretense of normalcy. My burden of secrecy was excruciating, but meditation became a precious respite. My greatest peace was on that cushion, following the breath and quieting mental chatter. In this twilight of our marriage, utterly exhausted, we finally gave up the façade. Jim came out openly and moved out of our home to a condominium of his own.

Two Vows

More than ever, I needed spiritual grounding. Meditating alone was helpful to calm my overwrought mind, but I sought deeper support of my practice. I had studied Pema Chödrön's books and had a great desire to learn from her in person. Dale Asrael orchestrated my first meeting with this remarkable teacher. At a week-long meditation retreat at Rocky Mountain Dharma Center, I met with Ani Pema for the first time and became her ardent student. The wisdom and kindness in her steady, matter-of-fact teachings and the clarity of her books grounded and assured me.

To become a Buddhist, one takes refuge in the Three Jewels: the Buddha, the dharma, and the sangha. It is a vow to do no harm, to rely on awakened nature, walking a path of loving-kindness and compassion. A refugee in Buddhism launches a unique, personal journey. I had already progressed through the thirteen weekends of Shambhala training and felt ready to formalize my conversion to Buddhism. Still, it was a momentous decision for me, a complete change in spiritual direction. After a sleepless night in 1994, I took the Refuge Vow with Ani Pema looking on and received my Buddhist name, *Pema Yudron*.

At first, the innocent "bright faith" of my youth was redirected to Pema as guru, a role she quickly denied. She carefully tutored me to let any idolization go. She was and is my *kalyanamitra*, my spiritual friend. Because of her gentle correction, I follow her teachings, but I don't deify her. This was a great lesson toward spiritual self-reliance. As time passed, I sometimes experienced doubt and fear and loneliness, but I also caught tantalizing glimpses of wholeness in my solitary way.

After spending all my early life immersed in church work and Christian fellowship, I had embraced a private spiritual practice in Buddhism. I loved the practice but eventually felt isolated. I had the teacher in the Buddha; I had the teachings in the dharma; but I didn't yet have the sangha, a spiritual community. I felt lonely in my practice. When Lucien Wulsin, chairman of the Naropa Board of Trustees, invited me to join their board, I accepted with gratitude. By then, I was quite comfortable at Naropa. I served as a trustee there from 1992 until 2000 (as Chairman of the Board for six of those years). Later, I returned for a second run as trustee from 2004 until 2008. Naropa became my sangha in those years.

In 2008, after nearly seventeen years as a Buddhist, I took the next step on my path. I studied root texts of the Bodhisattva Vow, the way of compassion in Mahayana practice. The classic guide for this path is the *Bodhicharyavatara,* an eighth-century Sanskrit text written by the Buddhist monk Shantideva. A 1996 English translation from the Tibetan outlines an ideal of love, compassion, generosity, and patience, with the intention to work for the deliverance of all beings. The task of the bodhisattva (literally "enlightenment being") is to demonstrate these qualities for the benefit of others. With guidance at another retreat taught by Pema Chödrön and close study of the poetic wording in this translation, I felt ready.

Witnessed by my meditation instructor, Acharya Dale Asrael, I took the Bodhisattva Vow: "And now, as long as space endures, as long as there are beings to be found, may I continue likewise to remain, to drive away the sorrows of the world." Inspired by this compassionate ideal of exchanging self for other, I vowed to hear the cries of the world and do my best to dispel the miseries of those I touch. This is the way of the bodhisattva.

Of course, in conventional terms, it is an impossible vow, an unattainable aspiration. Individual practitioners must interpret its meaning in the context of their circumstances. My understanding is this: intention counts. All sentient beings are interconnected; all are part of the Whole. Because everything is interrelated, we can never know how our actions touch and affect others, but each act of kindness does have an effect. My aspiration and daily intention is to serve and comfort others, doing what I can, with what I have, where I am. Perfection is beyond reach, but I believe that our efforts do make a difference, however hidden, however small.

Skillful Doubt

Buddhist practice satisfied most of my spiritual needs, but I did experience intermittent fear that I had made a wrong turn. I sometimes missed the sense of community that I had known within the church. During two different periods of paralyzing doubt, I retreated to familiar surroundings in the congregation of Columbine Unity Church. The humanistic messages at Unity differed greatly from the fundamental Christian teachings of my youth, and there was no taint of fundamentalist fervor. Sitting in a pew on Sunday mornings, I felt some comfort from familiar rituals of congregational singing, talks from the pastor, and the presence of others engaged in the same activities. I felt less isolated. For short periods of time, I successfully balanced my secluded Buddhist practice with habitual Unity ritual. But my heart remained on the meditation cushion, and I never fully integrated into that church community. I laid heavy guilt on myself for my ambivalence and eventually determined that I had to choose between the two traditions. Once again, I chose Buddhism.

Creating Sangha

In 2011 I brought together a small group of like-minded women with serious interest in studying the dharma. Since that time, we have continued to meet in my home on Sunday afternoons for meditation, followed by focused discussion of books by leading Buddhist teachers. Together, we have explored the nuanced interpretations of Pema Chödrön, Thich Nhat Hanh, Jack Kornfield, Sharon Salzberg, Ram Dass, Ezra Bayda, and many others. This regular gathering of *kalyanamitra*, spiritual friends, takes us ever deeper into the principles by which we live. It has become my essential sangha and satisfies the longing for spiritual community.

Despite this commitment, one question has recurred. For years, my Buddhist practice was periodically disturbed by the *God* question. Buddhism is "nontheistic." My teachers told me, "It just doesn't come up." Well, for me, God *did* come up. While the Refuge Vow opened a promising pattern of meditation practice and the Bodhisattva Vow encouraged compassionate service, a fundamental question of the *object of faith* arose. If I no longer believe in an anthropomorphic, paternal God, what do I believe in? I have a devotional nature, but I could not articulate a satisfying answer to "faith in what?" Early experience in the Christian church required unquestioned belief in a dogma prescribed from the *outside*. But heartfelt faith must come from *within* to unlock direct engagement in life, moment to moment. Such faith grows and changes, just as life does, but I still felt unclear about a supreme deity.

Over time, I began to understand my recurrent need to drop in and out of church. It was fear-driven. The curse of eternal damnation in a fiery hell is not inviting. However, skillful doubt eventually clarified understanding. If faith is willingness to engage life, then I had actually *practiced* my faith by dipping in and out of Unity and by asking hard questions. I opened my heart and mind through such periods of doubt but always reclaimed Buddhism. These explorations verified my conversion.

Coming to Peace

Heartened by the conviction that intention counts and that any action affects the entire universe, I am at last coming to peace with my overriding question about faith—what theologian Paul Tillich calls the "centering point for our life" and Sharon Salzberg terms our "ultimate concern." Evolving spiritual practice offers a sense of purpose and ethical grounding. I have been heavily influenced by Pema Chödrön's explication of Shantideva's *Bodhicharyavatara* and the diverse dharma books explored by my Sunday afternoon sangha. My centering point is the Bodhisattva Vow's essential requirement: service, exchanging self for other through acts of kindness.

Thich Nhat Hanh asserts that *inter-being* is the true human condition and that all is one. That makes us all equally precious, however insignificant we may feel. All beings—people, animals, trees and plants, flowing rivers and oceans, everything on the planet and in the uncounted universes—*everything* is part of the One, the Whole, the Ultimate, the Absolute, the Spirit that pervades all that is. Absolutely everything is connected. Tibetans call this unifying spirit Basic Goodness; Thich Nhat Hanh terms it True Nature or Buddha Nature; science refers to energy that manifests and changes but does not end. I cannot name it, for it is ineffable, but I believe in this all-pervasive Energy of creation that has existed from the beginning of time through this moment, encompassing all of life. When I try to describe or picture this ultimate Energy, my image is the vast, blue sky—indescribable space. Buddhism is nontheistic, but it is not atheistic. My concept of God has grown from a "heavenly Father" to an all-pervasive, everlasting Energy that connects every living and non-living person and thing. In that I have faith.

Experiences come to us—troubles, doubts, fears, mishaps, and tragedies. We also encounter ecstatic joy, comfort, plenty, quiet mind, peaceful moments, and steadfast love. These experiences come, then go. Every human event is part of this juicy, surprising existence, and every happening is ephemeral, like a cloud, passing through the infinite sky. This constant process that is the movement of life is called *impermanence*. "This, too, shall pass" is true of each experience, and each one is a minute part of eternal reality. Everything that exists will pass away, transform, and reemerge in its own time, for life is a continuation. Energy manifests, continues for a time, returns to its source, and reappears in a different form. In this way, life never ends, and death and fear are myths.

In *No Death, No Fear,* Thich Nhat Hanh offers a striking metaphor to clarify impermanence, manifestation, and continuation. We can see individual ocean waves going up and down. A wave rises above the surface, stands high a moment, then bends down and disappears. It may be tall or small. The wave has a beginning and end, emergence and decline, but its nature is always water. It has arrived at its destination and is at home in the wholeness of the ocean. We are like the wave; we are what we seek. Thich Nhat Hanh concludes, "You are what you are looking for. You are already what you want to become."

Recognizing our oneness with the Whole encourages a strong, self-reliant confidence during life's journey. Such abiding faith cannot be handed to us by anyone else, no matter how revered or trusted. We must discover it on our own. Joseph Campbell observed that we recover the treasures of life by going down into the abyss. "Where you stumble," he said, "there lies your treasure." We must rely on direct experience to determine individual truth. Skillful doubt was necessary to verify the faith I discovered.

Commitment to Path

The only way out of pain is to go through it. This was my stabilizing discovery. By coming back to the present moment, again and again, I found a passage. In fact, I began to understand deeply that *all* beings suffer and that even suffering is impermanent. It passes. The cause of much human anguish is clinging, craving, desire, hope for change, and fear of the future. Relief only comes when we let go of both hope and fear regarding these desires, see each experience as a teacher, as "fuel for waking up."

Legend has it that the Buddha's final words were Ehi passiko: "Come, see for yourself." My interpretation of this teaching is that there is no savior, no hand to hold, no infallible authority. Enlightenment is up to us, to be discovered in the direct experience of everyday life. Through years of meditative practice, I have begun to grasp that this is what being a Buddhist means to me: my life *is* my practice.

In these past years, I have experienced momentous life changes: finalizing my divorce from Jim, sale of our staffing business, tumultuous remarriage, developing a new vocation as a writer, deaths of loved ones, family concerns, finally enjoying a satisfying, committed companionship with my husband, Dale. Our evolving intimate partnership is a laboratory for the path to enlightenment. Successes and vicissitudes of ordinary existence have tested and confirmed the value of connecting in each passing moment with the natural flow of life and its impermanence. Staying present, looking deeply, opening to new possibilities, one simply continues on, taking the next breath.

In her book *Faith*, Salzberg wrote, life is "a vast fabric made of an evanescent, fleeting, shimmering pattern of turnings." It is true that every important change in my spiritual understanding has come as a result of a major turning point, such as our move to Boulder, with its rich stew of numinous investigation. The most disruptive, obviously, was Jim's coming out. That specific event precipitated my original conversion to Buddhism, the most significant decision of my lifetime.

This accounting of my faith journey only partially captures its many intersections and detours. Personal beliefs continue to evolve. For now, my concept of faith is a synthesis, in my individual consciousness, of Eastern and Western ideals, informing a personal philosophy. Continuing on a path of mindfulness and service, I simply need to take the next step in peace and love—and then the next. The process is benevolent, and that's all I need to know.

Rooted

Tangled twigs writhe in winds
swing wide in crazed dance
black against a dawning sky.
Gusts sing tenor notes,
stark above a low bass hum.
Framed by my window

wind-torn branches
mirror gale-tossed thoughts—
moody, serene, wild or wise,
seldom at rest.

Even tree trunks sway,
sturdiness challenged
by winter's screaming assault.
In anxious nights
they lean, then resist.

Odd to be quiet indoors
crossed legs planted
on familiar cushion.
Sit and breathe stillness,
silence draped like a cloak.

Votive flame's soothing sway
measures waltz tempo
undaunted by blustery blast
as the dance continues
placidly undisturbed.
Clamor without, quiet within.
Gust by gust, breath by breath,
stately trees and I survive.
Profoundly grounded, inside and out
roots reach wide, defy our storms.

No Baggage

I PICK MY WAY THROUGH A GRASSY FIELD OUTSIDE A SMALL *community north of Boulder. I've abandoned my car in a parking lot at the edge of town. I won't be needing it anymore. Taking a deep breath, I leave the sidewalk and pavement behind, feeling soft earth underfoot. The grass I'm walking through is long and fresh, stirring in the wind, and I notice its graceful waves and heady scent. Just ahead, up a low hill, railroad tracks shine in the warm autumn sun. I know that the train I'm meeting will stop at this crossing, and I can catch it here.*

The train is coming! Catching sight of it in the distance, I walk faster. It's good that I have no suitcase or purse or anything to slow me down. I cross the tracks to the other side, where the door can open for me. Breathless, I smooth my skirt and watch the train's approach. Despite my hurried walk, I feel fresh and clean—excited.

The train stops, the door slides open, and I step high to clamber aboard. I don't know where this train is going or where it will stop, but I feel elated, thrilled by the company I know I'll find here. I picture my teacher's broad smile and wise countenance, confident that she'll hold space for me as we travel. Walking through, from one car to the next, I notice that the aisle is narrow, as in a subway or commuter train. The seats are long benches facing each other, stretching the length of the cars, close enough to converse across the aisle. I pass through several cars, nodding at friendly passengers, feeling kinship with each one.

Reaching the last car of the train, I find the seat saved for me. With gratitude, I sit down beside my beloved kalyanamitra, Ani Pema Chödrön. She's engaged in quiet conversation with a woman facing us across the aisle. Pema scoots over a little to make room for me, and I settle into my seat at her right, a little breathless but feeling blissful. Though she's thin and aged, her smile is as fresh as an open sunflower. She's dressed, as always, in her flowing maroon Tibetan nun's robes, her white collar and saffron dickey freshly ironed, her hair shorn to less than an inch.

She turns back to her friend across the aisle and resumes their previous conversation. She obviously knows this lady, probably another of her multitude of students. Though the train car is full, they speak freely, trusting those around them. Others nearby listen and nod with empathy. The woman details her recovery from a serious loss, assuring Pema that she's now finally whole. I am certain that everyone on this train has suffered sickness and overcome grief. We have lived life! Now we are all going in the same direction.

I ride in silence and utter peace, feeling heart connection with the lady across the aisle and with everyone else here. I'm on the train with my teacher, humbled by the opportunity to be her friend, ready to serve where I can, and serene in the knowledge that I'm at last going in the right direction. This train will deliver me and my fellow passengers to our true destination. Unencumbered, with no baggage, I have everything I need to arrive safely, and I don't have to know exactly where that will be. I'm going home with Pema.

Despite two decades as a student of Buddhism, I still comprehend only small pieces of ultimate reality, like an unworked puzzle or a bag of mosaic tiles, yet to be assembled into a complete pattern. Questions still emerge. What actually happens after we die? When this body disintegrates, what comes next? Does the Buddhist principle of no-separate-self mean utter annihilation at the moment of death, extinction, like a candle snuffed out? Or is there some other plane of existence and, if so, what might it be like? These are recurring questions, as I age and move inexorably toward death.

A vivid nighttime dream, like this one, sometimes reveals more truth than conscious, intellectual study. Weeks after the dream, I awoke to an insightful interpretation. It was on Bodhi Day, December 8, traditionally celebrated to commemorate the moment of enlightenment by the historical Buddha, Siddhartha Gautama. The Sanskrit word, *bodhi,* literally means *awakened.* Though I had never observed Bodhi Day before, I woke that morning with a clear sense that something significant had shifted. Recent study had melded overnight, and I felt fresh assurance.

Thich Nhat Hanh's teaching on inter-being came to life in his vibrant metaphor of a wave in water. Never disconnected from its source, the wave is always part of the greater whole, having individuated only momentarily. Like that wave, people experience *relative* reality during a brief lifetime, in this body, time, and place. When we die, we return to our *absolute* reality, the Whole. In an ineffable, unconditioned awareness of interconnection with all that is, we can completely let go. We can stop clinging to the personality, the ego, and all other illusions. There is no further striving, no attachment, only liberation and utter freedom. This must be Nirvana.

My train dream was a vision of these convictions. Every detail is important—the waving grass, my car left behind, no purse or baggage, a special seat saved on the last train car, the sense of kinship with the other passengers, and the luminous presence of the teacher. I let go of the material world, leaving formerly valued possessions for someone else's use. The fresh grass waving around me recalls brief connection with the natural beauty and abundance of this world. Simple garments and no baggage suggest liberation from mundane needs. The train itself provides carefree transport, its open spaces filled with caring connections. I sit beside my teacher, who long ago introduced me to this life path and who gave me her own dharma name, *Pema*. Though my final destination is unclear, I continue the journey, fearlessly.

Moving from doubt to disbelief in my childhood religion, I first discovered Buddhism twenty-five years ago. Studying the dharma with Ani Pema and other gifted teachers, I embraced its compassionate teachings. I grew certain that suffering is inevitable, yet every life event, no matter how harsh, can be regarded as a teacher. "When the student is ready, the teacher appears." A remedy for suffering is to meet it with courageous patience, practice non-attachment, and then let it go. It is all impermanent. Buddhism became my wholesome guide for fulfilled living on a path of service.

Growing The Lotus

As the moon sets in the West
strike the match, touch the wick
candle flickers, licks shadows.
Incense rises, senses awake.
The Buddha smiles, image of calm.
Strike the gong, mellow tone,
bow with inborn dignity.
Ancient ritual, familiar chants
mind prepared for peace.
On the cushion, erect, awake,
touch rising thought, let it go.
Fully present, sit in inner space.
Breath by breath, in and out
dissolve in the Whole.
Day after day, learn to stay.
In shrine room hush, the lotus grows.
Born in the mud, it reaches for light.

ABOUT THE AUTHOR

CAROL GREVER HAS BEEN A SUCCESSFUL BUSINESSWOMAN, English professor, and community advocate. She now writes professionally. She authored three nonfiction books, *My Husband Is Gay*, *When Your Spouse Comes Out*, and *Memory Quilt*, and produced an award-winning documentary, *One Gay, One Straight: Complicated Marriages*. *Glimpses*, her full-length poetry collection, won the Colorado Authors' League 2013 Prize. As a recognized spokesperson on straight spouse issues, she has appeared on major network TV shows, including *Anderson Cooper 360*, *The Early Show*, *Good Morning America*, and *The Oprah Winfrey Show*, and has done media interviews on three continents. Read more about her work at **www.carolgrever.com**